THE

oracle
diet

MICHAEL VAN STRATEN

THE oracle diet

MICHAEL VAN STRATEN

Recipes by Sally Pearce and Michael van Straten

KYLE CATHIE LTD

contents

introduction

The ORACle Diet is unique among modern health and food books. It's about eating and enjoying delicious meals. It's about optimal nutrition and minimal fuss. It's about maximum benefit and the least possible damage to your body. It's about pleasure, not guilt.

The way we eat has changed more in the last 100 years than in the previous 100,000 – and I've watched in horror how these changes have accelerated during the 40 years since I first became involved in complementary medicine. As a naturopath, I use nutrition as the platform on which all health is based. Without good food, there can never be good health. But the combination of changing lifestyles, lack of skills in the kitchen, increasing time pressures and the determined efforts of the food manufacturing industry have pushed us into a violent vortex of ever-decreasing nutritional value and ever-increasing consumption of health-damaging foods.

There's no doubt that freezers, microwaves and instant meals have brought convenience to everyday living. But at what price? In spite of ever-increasing affluence, dramatic advances in medicine and the ability of surgeons to replace most parts of the body with donor organs or artificial implants, health in the Western world is in steep decline. It's true that we've conquered smallpox and the plague. There are vaccines to protect children and adults from many communicable diseases, drugs that control blood pressure and diabetes, scanners to detect the tiniest changes deep within the body and ever more successful treatments for many types of cancer.

Nonetheless, health-care services are collapsing under the pressure of demand always exceeding supply. Someone in the UK dies prematurely of heart disease every three minutes. Sperm counts have halved in the last fifty years, and infertility problems have soared. An increasing number of our children are obese. Allergies such as asthma, eczema and hay fever are ten times more common than thirty years ago. And when life expectancy is increasing and more people are retiring early, these golden years are plagued by diabetes, arthritis, poor eyesight, osteoporosis and Alzheimer's disease.

You may find it hard to believe, but your food – and the food you give your children – holds the key to the prevention or reduced risk or impact of most of these problems. Scientists have known for decades that the essential vitamins, minerals and trace elements play a vital role in both the preservation of life and the maintenance of good health, but it's only in recent years that the overwhelming importance of anti-oxidants has been acknowledged. It's these protective chemicals that fight against the damaging free radicals that attack cells throughout the body.

The ORACle Diet is a delicious way of eating, a natural path to health and vitality, dramatically increased chances of disease-free progression into maturity and the simplest possible way of adding years to your life and life to your years.

It's time to stop worrying and love your food

Helena Rubenstein, the great pioneer of the cosmetics industry, said you should never put anything on your face that you wouldn't put in your mouth, and how right she was. No amount of expensive lotions and potions will help stave off the relentless march of time and ageing unless you're eating the right foods. And the key anti-ageing foods are fruits and vegetables.

Medical science has conquered the ravages of most infectious diseases, surgeons can give you a new heart or a new hip, drugs can keep you mobile as the joints begin to stiffen, sewage systems and safe drinking water have eradicated killer epidemics of dysentery and typhoid in the Western world, but all this is papering over the cracks. Ageing is a relentless march of nutritional deficiencies and in spite of worldwide population studies and major research in the most prestigious university laboratories, the medical profession in general ignores the relevance of nutrition and its anti-ageing function.

It's simple: every one of you can slow down and even reverse many of the body's natural ageing processes, and you'll not only feel better and look better, but you'll gain enormous protection against the scourges of heart disease and some cancers. All you have to do is eat more of the very specific foods that are richest in nature's defensive chemicals, the antioxidants.

Fighting free radicals

Oxidation is a damaging process caused by a group of chemicals called free radicals, which are produced mainly when the body burns up the oxygen we breathe to keep us alive. We're also subject to damaging free radicals that get into our system from the outside as a result of smoking, environmental pollution, radiation, too much sunlight, and irritant chemicals that make contact with our skin. These free radicals are the very core of the ageing process, destroying our body cells one by one.

One of the world's leading nutritionists, Dr Venket Rao, Professor Emeritus of Nutritional Sciences at the Faculty of Medicine, University of Toronto, has been studying the role of antioxidants and their availability to the body's cells since 1997. When I met him recently he said:

'We have repeatedly shown that the protective anti-oxidants are only valuable if they are biologically available to the body's cells. Oxidative damage is just like rust on a piece of iron. If you coat the iron with an antioxidant, the surface remains perfect. In the body antioxidants have the same protective effect on every individual cell. We've studied chemically induced cancers in human colon cells, bone loss, prostate cancer cells, breast cancer cells and long-term dietary intervention in both bone health and prostate patients, and in all these areas the role of antioxidants like lycopene have been proved extremely effective.'

Using Professor Rao's analogy, just think what happens to your wrought-iron garden gate if you don't paint it regularly. The paint flakes off, leaving the iron exposed to the air, and the oxygen attacks, making the gate rust. In time, the rust damages the metal and the gate starts to disintegrate. Exactly the same thing happens in the human body. Free radicals circulate through our bodies constantly, looking for healthy cells to latch on to and attack. They aren't choosy about the cells they injure – lungs or liver, stomach or skin, heart or arteries – they'll have a go at anything.

Our only protection is to stop them dead in their tracks and neutralise their destructive potential. The antioxidant chemicals that we get from food are the body's natural police force, patrolling every nook and cranny on their seek-and-destroy journey. If there aren't enough antioxidants, the free radicals win and you suffer premature ageing and disease.

The early research into antioxidants focused on specific components of food: vitamins A, C and E; protective chemicals that were isolated from red wine, broccoli and cabbages; and carotenoids from carrots, spinach and greens. It wasn't long before antioxidant pills made with these ingredients appeared on the market, but pills were only half the story. Even in controlled laboratory experiments, using specific antioxidants did not produce nearly such good results as using fresh fruits and vegetables.

So where do we find the foods richest in these miracle chemicals? You find them at the greengrocer, in the street market, in your corner shop, in the supermarket or they may even be in your own back garden. They are simple, everyday, inexpensive fruits and vegetables. Of course all fruits and vegetables are good sources of vitamins such as A, C and E, but those that are deeply coloured – dark green, deep red, purple, yellow and bright orange – tend to have the highest levels of vitamins and minerals.

The antioxidant properties in the pigments that colour these wonderful foods are your best weapon against ageing. Researchers have identified around 2,000

different pigments in plants, including 450 different carotenoids and 150 anthocyanidins. These are part of a family of chemicals called polyphenols, which form the most powerfully protective group of natural food chemicals. When there are such vast numbers of important substances, it's obvious that taking pills that contain just a few of the antioxidants is no match for eating complete foods that have them all – though there are specific substances like betacarotene for the lungs, lycopene for heart and prostate, and lutein and xeaxanthine for eye protection that are valuable supplements.

The ORAC score

The US Department of Agriculture Human Nutrition Research Center on Ageing (HNRCA) at Tufts University in Boston, Massachusetts, has been studying the role of antioxidants for some years now. Because large trials with specific antioxidant vitamins had not been conclusive, scientist Ron Prior and his colleagues decided to examine the antioxidant properties of whole foods. In their natural state, plants contain more than 4,000 potential antioxidant chemicals, and there is strong evidence that these are protective against many life-threatening conditions. Just one study – of 1,300 elderly people in Massachusetts –

showed that those who had two or more portions a day of dark green and yellow vegetables were only half as likely to suffer a fatal heart attack, and had a third of the risk of dying of cancer compared with people averaging less than one portion a day.

As always in nature, there is a synergistic benefit from the interaction of all the phytochemicals in the plants we consume, and Prior and his team set out to measure the total antioxidant powers of individual foods. They established the oxygen radical absorbance capacity – the ORAC score – a measure of each food's ability to neutralise free radicals and protect the body from ageing, heart disease, cancer and other degenerative conditions. All plant foods are a source of ORAC, and that includes whole grains, nuts, seeds and beans as well as fruits and vegetables. Meat, fish and dairy products have other vital nutritional roles, but do not have a significant ORAC value. The highest scores are found in the most colourful produce, such as blueberries, blackberries, cranberries, kale, strawberries, spinach, Brussels sprouts, beetroot and sweet potatoes – not surprisingly, dried fruits, with all the water removed, are weight for weight the richest of all.

The HNRCA has produced a league table of high-ORAC foods.

Fruit or vegetable ORAC per 100g (3¹/₂oz)

Prunes (dried plums)	5,770		Sweetcorn	400
Raisins	2,830		Aubergines	390
Blueberries	2,400		Cauliflower	377
Blackberries	2,036		Peas, fresh or frozen	364
Garlic	1,939		Potatoes	313
Kale	1,770		Sweet potatoes	301
Cranberries	1,750		Cabbage, raw	298
Strawberries	1,540		Leaf lettuce	262
Spinach	1,260		Cantaloupe melon	252
Raspberries	1,220		Bananas	221
Brussels sprouts	980		Apples	218
Plums	949		Tofu	213
Alfalfa sprouts	930		Carrots	207
Broccoli	890		Stringless (green) beans	201
Beetroot	840		Tomatoes	189
Avocado	782		Courgettes	176
Oranges	750		Apricots	164
Red grapes	739		Peaches	158
Red peppers	710		Squash, yellow	150
Cherries	670		Lima beans	136
Kiwi	602		Pears	134
Baked beans	503		Iceberg lettuce	116
Pink grapefruit	483		Watermelon	104
Kidney beans	460		Honeydew melon	97
Onion	450		Celery	61
White grapes	446		Cucumber	54

My analysis of hundreds of my patients' diets over the last few years shows that their average daily intake of ORAC units is just over 1,000 and even those on otherwise healthy diets tend to consume far more of the low-ORAC fruits and vegetables. Although these provide adequate supplies of vitamins and minerals, they won't produce the maximum anti-ageing and protective potential of the high-ORAC foods. According to Prior, we should all be aiming for at least 3,000 and, for maximum protection, 5,000 ORAC units every single day. This is the amount your body needs in order to raise the levels of antioxidant protection for every vulnerable cell.

Consistently eating sufficient quantities of high-ORAC foods increases the antioxidant effectiveness of your blood by up to 25 per cent. It protects the heart, arteries and tiniest capillaries of the circulatory system. It slows down ageing in the skin. It prolongs effective mental functions and may protect against Alzheimer's disease, MS and Parkinson's. Most dramatically, following the ORACle Diet will, without doubt, help your body in its natural fight against the ravages of cancer.

All of these foods, in addition to their high-ORAC value and their key anti-ageing properties, are also some of the richest sources of other nutrients: folic acid in kale, spinach, Brussels sprouts and broccoli; vitamin C in blueberries, blackberries, strawberries, raspberries, red peppers, oranges, cherries and kiwis; vitamin E in blackberries, spinach, alfalfa sprouts and avocado; iron in prunes, raisins, spinach and beetroot; bioflavonoids in pink grapefruit, oranges and cherries; natural antiseptics and antifungals in onions and garlic, which also have cholesterol-lowering properties.

But is it easier to get all the nutrients you need from pills?

Supplements: do you need them?

At a time when everyone talks about the importance of vitamins and minerals, and they're even listed on your breakfast cereal packet, it's hard to believe that it's less than a hundred years since Casimir Funk and Sir Frederick Gowland first discovered these essential micronutrients. Now, in the twenty-first century, the shelves in health stores, pharmacies and supermarkets groan under a vast array of supplements.

Multivitamins, single vitamins, megadose mixtures, pills, capsules, elixirs and combinations for almost any illness you can think of … there are so many variations it's not surprising that people leave the shop confused and empty-handed.

But do you need them anyway?

The answer for a lot of you will be yes – in spite of the fact that most doctors will tell you that you get all you need from your food. In an ideal world, where everyone ate a balanced diet of fresh, home-made meals and used mainly organic ingredients, few of you would benefit from supplements. But the truth is very different.

A recent survey of 800 people in 500 households in Britain revealed that the diets of 93 per cent of men and 98 per cent of women between the ages of 18 and 54 were deficient in folic acid, 60 per cent of women were getting too little iron, 90 per cent of men and women were getting insufficient amounts of vitamin B6, 73 per cent of women were getting less than their minimum requirement of calcium and 50 per cent of them weren't getting enough zinc.

I analyse the diets of several hundred patients every year and hardly any of them get enough of all the essential nutrients to meet the minimum daily requirements. They're also commonly short of selenium, iodine, and vitamins E and D. Even the vital vitamin C is often deficient in the diets of men, women and children.

These nutrient deficiencies can have a devastating effect on health. Many of the world's leading nutritionists believe that although the recommended daily allowances (RDAs) may be enough to prevent deficiency diseases like scurvy, rickets or beriberi, they're far too low to promote optimum health and protect against disease in general.

Even assuming you get enough nutrients in your food, there are other factors that may stop you absorbing many of them. For example, spinach is rich in calcium, but because spinach contains chemicals called oxalates, you'll be lucky if 5 per cent of it is absorbed. If you take a large dose of iron, zinc, magnesium or calcium, it can reduce the absorption of the others and mean you need more of them, too.

Eating lots of wholegrain cereals, bran and soy products can also reduce absorption of minerals. And the chemicals in spinach, beetroot, rhubarb, gooseberries and chocolate block the absorption of calcium and iron; strong tea contains tannins, which also interfere with iron absorption. It doesn't help if you switch to coffee, as caffeine is a diuretic and makes you lose calcium in your urine. Studies have shown a direct link between coffee drinking and loss of bone density, so it's a good idea to have your morning cereal with milk or your calcium tablet an hour after your first morning coffee.

Phosphorous is another mineral essential for bones, but getting too much of it from cola drinks increases the body's loss of calcium.

Taking huge doses of vitamins isn't the answer either: the more you take, the less your body can absorb. In small doses of vitamin B12, for instance, 70 per cent is absorbed, but if you take more than you need, the amount your body actually gets can range from nothing to 50 per cent. The same is true for most other B vitamins and vitamin C.

Because zinc is known to help with colds and male fertility, it has become extremely popular as a supplement, but excessive amounts can reduce the quantity of copper in the body and that can lower the levels of the good HDL-cholesterol in your blood.

One much ignored and little understood area is the really bad effects that many prescribed medicines have on nutritional status. These include appetite-suppressants; chemotherapy, which causes nausea or vomiting; laxatives, which reduce all nutrient absorption; aluminium-based antacids, which interfere with the absorption of phosphorus; some epilepsy medications, which can affect folic acid absorption and cause anaemia; and cholesterol-lowering drugs, which can reduce the body's levels of vitamins A, D, E and K.

Antibiotics can also kill the good bugs responsible for producing B vitamins. The Pill may reduce levels of B6, and diuretics could make you lose potassium, essential for all muscles, including the heart. These reactions can be more worrying in people who have a poor diet to start with or serious health problems and in growing children.

Those people who will certainly need to supplement their diets are those who are physically very active, like athletes and dancers – and, worryingly, children and adolescents who live on junk food and refuse all efforts to persuade them to eat fruit and vegetables. Anyone preparing for or recovering from surgery or recuperating from any acute illness, pregnant or breast-feeding women, individuals with stressful personal or business lives and people with any chronic bowel disorder will also require supplements.

People with mouth or throat problems that prevent normal eating, women past the menopause and, of course, the elderly, whose digestive systems are less efficient and who tend to eat less anyway, are candidates too. Obviously, supplements are essential in the treatment of eating disorders and for anyone else whose life is so haphazard that regular eating is impossible.

So of course vitamin, mineral and nutritional pills have an important role to play, but far too many people treat them as substitutes for food rather than supplements to a healthy diet. The simple truth is that no one can live on a junk food diet, take a pill and expect to be healthy.

Food – the secret of youth

There is already a substantial growth in the number of people taking early retirement and as the population continues to age many of us will have the opportunity to enjoy 25 –30 years of leisure. I suspect that a huge proportion of people will be able to take advantage of the employment situation and take on some part-time work for the mental stimulus as well as the extra money that this could provide during these golden years. But to give this period of your life the fullest sense of well-being and enjoyment, you need to be healthy.

You don't need a revolution in your eating, you don't need rigid or peculiar diets, you certainly don't need expensive pills and potions – just lots of the foods that look good, taste good and will do you the ultimate good. These are the foods that will prolong your active years, something that's becoming more important than ever as life expectancy increases and modern medicine extends its ability to keep us alive. Of course there are no miracle answers but if you follow the immensely enjoyable ORACle Diet, you give the odds for healthy living an enormous boost in your favour.

Everyone must now know that five portions of fruit and vegetables a day – totalling approximately 500g (1lb) in weight – is the minimum quantity needed for a well-balanced and healthy diet. But if you really want to beat the ageing process and achieve maximum health protection, make it seven portions, at least three of which come from the high-ORAC list. It really is easier than you think. Each of these delicious mixtures will give you optimum high-ORAC protection on a daily basis:

o 50g (2oz) prunes, and 1 tablespoon each of blueberries and raisins with your breakfast cereal, or

o 75g (3oz) spinach, 75g (3oz) Brussels sprouts, and a salad with $^1/_2$ red pepper, 1 tablespoon of alfalfa sprouts and 1 tablespoon of broccoli florets with your midday meal, or

o 75g (3oz) cooked baby beetroot, a large red pepper stuffed with sweetcorn, chopped onion and raisins, and a bowl of cherries or strawberries with your evening meal

Boost your levels even more by eating California ready-to-eat prunes and raisins as between meal nibbles during the day.

The high-ORAC guide is your chance to protect your body from the visible and invisible effects of ageing. You can slow down the development of wrinkles and old-looking, pitted skin. Protect your joints from arthritis, protect your nervous system from early dementia and senility. Reduce your risks of heart disease and increase your chances of avoiding many forms of cancer. All you have to do is make sure that your nutritional bank balance is always in the red, blue, yellow, orange and green. This is the food rainbow that will colour you healthy.

This must be the simplest and most enjoyable prescription for health and long life that has ever been devised. Each recipe in this book has a star rating, and each star represents 1,000 ORAC units. Take a quick look at the recipes and menus and you'll see how incredibly easy it is to reach and exceed the optimum 5,000. Don't forget that fruit and vegetable juices are excellent ORAC sources too, and provide almost the same score as whole produce.

You may be surprised that in a healthy-eating book there are no prohibitions or dire warnings about fat, calories, carbohydrates or treats. The reason there aren't is not because you can push up your ORACs, stuff yourself with burgers, chips and chocolates and still expect to reap all the benefits. The fact is, by increasing the amount of plant foods in your diet you will automatically push out a lot of the less healthy foods. It's also important that we all get back to the joy of eating and stop equating pleasure with sin.

Food is not just fuel. It's there to be relished, enjoyed and, whenever possible, eaten in the good company of friends and family. It's part of the cement that binds social groups together, part of the social structure that helps children learn how to communicate and, just as importantly, acquire both knowledge and love of food and cooking.

Where your food is concerned, it's what you do most of the time that matters to your health and well-being. What you do occasionally doesn't matter at all.

Enjoy and be well!

breakfasts

All recipes in this chapter serve 2

ORAC value per serving ★★★★★★✓

porridge with prunes and apricots

The hardy Scots have known for centuries that porridge is the best possible start to the day – and how right they are! Protein, B vitamins and slow-release energy make this the perfect breakfast. But when you add the dried fruit in this recipe, you get the additional protective benefits of a truly huge ORAC score.

2 average-size cups good organic porridge oats
2 average-size cups milk
2 average-size cups water
8 ready-to-eat or semi-dried prunes
8 ready-to-eat or semi-dried apricots
2 teaspoons organic brown granulated sugar
Extra milk for drizzling

1 Put the porridge oats into a saucepan.

2 Add the milk and water, and bring to a gentle simmer, stirring occasionally. Cook for 5 minutes or as directed on the porridge packet, adding more milk if the mixture gets too thick.

3 Meanwhile, snip the prunes and apricots to the size of half a teaspoon and add them to the cooked porridge. Cover and leave for 1 minute.

4 Pour into two bowls, sprinkle the sugar on top and leave to melt – about 1 minute.

5 Serve with the extra milk poured on top.

ORAC value per serving ★★★

fruity starter with a poach-up

This is a terrific breakfast, which provides you with four times as much vitamin C as you need for a whole day, 20 per cent of your calcium needs, plenty of protein from the beans and wholemeal bread, and the special type of soluble fibre that all beans contain, which helps lower the cholesterol in your blood. All this before you even think about its super ORAC score.

1 large pink grapefruit
4 kiwi fruit, peeled and sliced
2 tablespoons yogurt sauce (see page 126)
2 pieces medium-sliced wholemeal bread
400g (14oz) canned organic baked beans
4 fresh tomatoes

1 Peel the grapefruit, leaving some of the pith attached to the flesh, and separate the segments.

2 Arrange the grapefruit and kiwi fruit around the perimeter of 2 plates and place the yogurt sauce in the middle. Serve while you cook the rest of the meal.

3 Put the tomatoes in one layer in a saucepan of water. Bring to the boil and cook until the skins begin to split – 3–5 minutes, depending on size – then strip the skins off.

4 Meanwhile, toast the bread and heat the beans.

5 Serve the tomatoes beside the beans heaped on the toast.

ORAC value per serving ★★✔

grorange juice, poached egg and poached tomato

Masses of vitamin C, lots of lycopene from the tomatoes for prostate- and breast-cancer protection; protein, iron and B vitamins from the eggs; and fibre from the wholemeal toast … what more could you ask for, apart from a brilliant helping of ORAC?

Juice of 4 large oranges, or shop-bought freshly squeezed juice
Juice of 1 grapefruit, or shop-bought freshly squeezed juice
1 teaspoon organic vinegar – the flavour doesn't matter
4 organic free-range eggs
4 tomatoes
2 slices wholemeal toast

1 Mix the juices in a jug and pour into 2 glasses.

2 Fill a large frying pan with water and bring to a simmer. (You may have to cook this breakfast in two batches if your frying pan isn't large enough.) Add the vinegar.

3 Roll the eggs, still in their shells, in the water for about 30 seconds (this keeps the whites together as they poach). Remove and set aside for another 30 seconds.

4 Add the tomatoes to the pan.

5 Break in the eggs and simmer for 4 minutes or until the egg yolks are as firm as you like and the tomato skins start to split.

6 Serve the eggs and tomatoes on slices of wholemeal toast.

ORAC value per serving   ★★✔

avocado with sliced tomato

Avocados are a source of one the healthiest of all oils – mono-unsaturated fat, which helps reduce cholesterol and blood pressure. They also contain a large amount of vitamin E, which protects the heart and blood vessels and is essential for clean, supple skin. With the vitamin C from tomatoes and lemon juice, this adds up to a slightly unusual, but extremely healthy, anti-ageing breakfast with a substantial protective ORAC score.

2 large, ripe, but not bruised, avocados, peeled and stoned
1 tablespoon lemon juice
2 slices wholemeal bread
4 tomatoes, sliced
Freshly ground black pepper

1 Mash the avocado flesh thoroughly.

2 Add the lemon juice, to prevent the avocado discolouring, and a few twists of freshly ground black pepper.

3 Toast the bread and heap on the avocado mash.

4 Serve with the sliced tomatoes on the side

`ORAC value per serving` ★✦

honeyed fruit and yogurt

Nothing could be quicker than this delicious summer breakfast. Lots of energy and potassium from the bananas; vitamin C from the raspberries; calcium, protein and immune-boosting good bacteria in the yogurt; and an instant lift from the honey. Perfect if you're going to the gym, for a run or a game of tennis – and a good start to your ORAC day.

2 bananas, peeled and sliced
150g (5oz) raspberries
300g (10oz) natural organic bio-yogurt
About 2 tablespoons honey, preferably organic

1 Divide the banana slices between 2 bowls.

2 Gently wash the raspberries, taking care not to bruise them, and pile on top of the bananas.

3 Tip half the yogurt on top of each bowl.

4 Drizzle with the honey.

`ORAC value per serving`   ★★★★★

swiss muesli with blueberries

The traditional Alpine start to the day and a far cry from the sawdust texture of cheap muesli with added milk eaten straightaway. Good muesli is made with oats and lots of raisins, sultanas and other dried fruits so you get instant energy from the fruit sugars, slow-release energy from the oats, calcium and beneficial bugs from the yogurt and a huge amount of vitamin C from the blueberries. This is another age-defying breakfast with an abundance of ORACs.

2 bowls half filled with good quality, unsweetened, preferably
*   organic muesli*
About 700ml (1 1/4 pints) organic apple juice
150ml (5oz) natural, full-fat, organic bio-yogurt
150g (5oz) fresh blueberries

1 The night before, pour the juice on to the muesli – it should almost drown it, as the cereal mix will nearly double in size – then stir in the yogurt.

2 In the morning, wash the blueberries carefully.

3 Serve the muesli with the blueberries piled on top.

ORAC value per serving ★★★★★★✦

devilled prunes with spicy tomato sauce

Definitely not a Monday morning breakfast – unless it's a bank holiday – but a perfect, leisurely weekend brunch. Traditionally, devils on horseback, made with kidneys, are served as a savoury after dinner in the upper-class gentlemen's clubs in London. They became a popular breakfast dish during the days of the Raj. Made here with prunes, they're as delicious as they are dramatically high in their ORAC score.

12 leaves flat-leaf parsley
12 large ready-to-eat stoneless prunes, washed and
*   thoroughly dried*
6 large rashers organic back bacon
1 quantity spicy tomato sauce (see page 123)

1 Place a parsley leaf on top of each prune.

2 Cut most of the fat off the bacon, stretch each rasher with the back of a wooden spatula and cut in half lengthways. Wrap the bacon around the prunes and parsley, and secure with half a cocktail stick.

3 Put the wrapped prunes on a grill rack under a medium grill, turning until the bacon is well cooked, but not crispy.

4 Serve with the tomato sauce.

ORAC value per serving ★★★★

fruit-filled melon shells

As breakfast, a starter, a dessert or a lunchtime snack, this is refreshing, tasty and unbelievably healthy. The melon provides lots of betacarotene, for eyes and skin, and all the berries will give you around five times the amount of vitamin C you need for one day. But the real gift from nature in this recipe is its staggeringly high ORAC score from such a small amount of food.

About 175g (6oz) of mixed strawberries, blueberries, blackberries
*   and redcurrants*
1 ripe cantaloupe melon, halved and deseeded

1 Wash the berries carefully, removing any hulls.

2 Wash the currants and strip them from their stalks, but don't bother to hull them – you'll still be there at lunchtime.

3 Heap the soft fruit into the hollows in the melon and serve.

ORAC value per serving ★★★★★★

compôte of dried fruits with yogurt and flax seeds

If you're in a hurry in the morning, this is the healthy alternative to stopping on the way to work for coffee and a doughnut. Prepared the night before, it will take less than five minutes to pour on the yogurt and eat – and it will help get your day off to a flying start. Energy, betacarotene, fibre, calcium and masses of vitamin E from the flax seeds are the extra rewards on top of a huge ORAC score.

350g (12oz) mixed dried fruits – prunes, apricots, mangos, raisins,
  blueberries, apples, bananas or any other that take your fancy
300g (10oz) natural bio-yogurt, preferably organic
2 tablespoons flax seeds

1 Put the fruit in a large bowl and cover with boiling water. Allow to cool, then put into the fridge overnight.

2 In the morning, drain the fruit. Serve the yoghurt on the side with the flax seeds scattered over. Arrange the fruit and yogurt on 2 plates and sprinkle the flax seeds on top.

ORAC value per serving   ★★

pink grapefruit and jugged kippers with gooseberry sauce

Kippers are a superb source of essential fatty acids and vitamin D. They also provide excellent protein and minerals, including iodine. Despite their salt content, they're a useful heart-protective food as long as you keep your overall salt consumption as low as possible. The gooseberry sauce is a luxury extra that will provide a valuable ORAC addition. Starting with pink grapefruit gives you lots of extra vitamin C and more ORAC.

1 large pink grapefruit
2 naturally smoked, undyed kippers
Gooseberry sauce (see page 124)

1 Halve and segment the grapefruit.

2 While you're eating your grapefruit starter, fill a large jug with freshly boiled water. Drop in the kippers, head-side down. Cover tightly with cooking foil and leave for 7 minutes.

3 Pull out the fish by their tails and allow any excess water to drain off. Serve with the sauce.

soups

All recipes in this chapter serve 4

ORAC value per 100ml ★

basic stock

In these days of instant stock cubes and 'fresh' stock on the supermarket shelves, the art of making stock is disappearing fast. I think that's a great shame, as none of the commercially-prepared stocks tastes as good as your own and they certainly don't have the ORAC value of this recipe. This stock is easy to make and freezes well – I turn it into ice cubes, which can then be used from frozen to enhance stews, casseroles, sauces and, of course, as the basis for any delicious soup. This is one kitchen skill that handsomely repays such a small investment in time and effort.

2 large onions
2 sticks celery with their leaves, washed
4 leeks, trimmed and washed
4 large carrots, trimmed and peeled
3 tomatoes, quartered
2 sprigs thyme
1 large sprig rosemary
2 bay leaves
6 peppercorns

1 Peel and slice 1 onion. Leave the other whole and unpeeled – the skin will give extra colour to the stock.

2 Put all the ingredients into a large saucepan with about 4 litres (7¼ pints) of water. A pasta or asparagus pan with an inside sieve is ideal.

3 Simmer gently without a lid for 2 hours. Remove the vegetables from the pan and push through a sieve into the stock.

ORAC value per serving ★↗

sweet potato and pear

This is a robust soup, which doesn't need liquidising, although I like to mash the pears and sweet potatoes gently with a fork before serving. As well as its benefits for anyone with urine infections (thanks to the cranberry juice) and its very high content of cancer-protective betacarotenes, it also has an unusual flavour and a high ORAC score.

2 tablespoons extra-virgin olive oil
1 large red onion or 2 smaller ones, chopped
4 sweet potatoes, peeled and cubed
5 conference pears, peeled, cored and cubed
250ml (9fl oz) cranberry juice
850ml (1½ pints) basic stock (see previous recipe)
½ teaspoon (preferably freshly) ground nutmeg
300g (10oz) natural bio-yogurt

1 Heat the oil in a large saucepan, add the onions and sauté gently for 5 minutes.

2 Add the sweet potatoes and pear to the pan with the cranberry juice and stock.

3 Bring to the boil and simmer for 45 minutes.

4 Crush the vegetables roughly with a potato masher.

5 Stir in the nutmeg and yogurt.

minty pea and sweetcorn

This wonderful summer soup takes little longer to prepare than opening and heating a can, or even worse, using one of the instant soup powders full of salt and chemicals. It's an interesting variation on ordinary pea soup, providing extra calcium from the fromage frais, a delicious creamy texture and a good ORAC score.

200g (7oz) frozen peas
200g (7oz) frozen sweetcorn
700ml (1¼ pints) basic stock (see page 30)
50g unsalted butter
6 large sprigs mint
300ml (½ pint) low-fat fromage frais
3 large sprigs fresh chervil or ½ teaspoon dried
Salt and pepper

1 Cook the peas and all but 4 tblspns of the sweetcorn in the stock with 2 sprigs of the mint until tender – about 5 minutes.

2 Stir in the fromage frais, fresh or dried chervil and 2 more mint sprigs, and heat gently for 2 minutes.

3 Whizz in batches in a blender until very smooth. Leave to cool, then put into the fridge to chill.

4 Check seasoning, adding freshly ground pepper or salt if necessary.

5 Sauté the reserved sweetcorn in the butter, scatter on top

6 Serve with remaining mint and chervil leaves (if you have them) floating on top.

ORAC value per serving ★★★

chilled avocado

A bowl of this will do more for your skin than a fortune's worth of fancy cosmetics. Anti-ageing, wrinkle-beating and highly protective against heart disease, circulation problems and cancer, the smooth, cool appearance belies the hot spiciness of these Mexican flavours. A single bowl is more than a half day's ORAC score.

5 ripe avocados
1 litre (1³/4 pints) chicken stock from the real chicken soup recipe (see page 40)
Juice of 1 large lemon
2 large garlic cloves, finely chopped
3 red chillies, deseeded and chopped
¹/4 teaspoon cayenne pepper
4 plump spring onions, roughly chopped
Leaves of 12 large stems coriander
200g (7oz) canned organic plum tomatoes, drained
150ml (5fl oz) natural organic bio-yogurt
4 tablespoons pumpkin seeds
Salt and pepper

1 Put the avocado flesh into a food processor with the chicken stock and add the lemon juice.

2 Add the garlic, chillies and cayenne pepper and blend until smooth.

3 Add the spring onions, coriander leaves and tomatoes, and process briefly again.

4 Add the yogurt and whizz for just a few seconds. Adjust the seasoning and leave in the fridge to chill.

5 Dry-fry the pumpkin seeds gently and allow to cool. Serve the soup with the pumpkin seeds floating on top.

ORAC value per serving ★★

carrot and coconut

This combination of mundane carrots and exotic coconut with the spiciness of coriander is reminiscent of tropical islands. For many people, just the smell of coconut makes them think of sunshine and blue seas. This soup will certainly put the sunshine back into your life.

2 tablespoons extra-virgin olive oil
1 large onion, finely chopped
900g (2lbs) carrots, finely cubed
¹/2 teaspoon ground coriander
700ml (1¹/4 pints) basic stock (see page 30)
400ml (14fl oz) canned coconut milk
2 sprigs fresh coriander
Salt and pepper

1 Heat the oil in a large saucepan, add the onion and sweat for 5 minutes.

2 Add the carrots to the pan with the ground coriander and continue cooking for 10 more minutes, stirring constantly.

3 Pour in the stock and coconut milk and simmer until the carrots are tender – this shouldn't take more than 10 minutes.

4 Whizz in a food processor until smooth, then reheat and season according to taste.

5 Tear the leaves from the coriander sprigs and serve the soup with the leaves floating on top.

ORAC value per serving ★★✦

cheat's gazpacho

Here's another summer favourite, which brings back memories of Spanish holidays. The best I've ever had was in a beach-side café at the southern resort of Nerja, and I only have to taste gazpacho to smell the wood fire under the chef's paella pan. This quick and easy version is equally delicious and overflows with age-defying ORAC properties.

1 red pepper, halved and deseeded
1 yellow pepper, halved and deseeded
1 large, sweet Spanish onion, finely chopped
3 garlic cloves, finely chopped
1 large tomato, roughly chopped
1 cucumber, peeled, halved and deseeded
Leaves of 5 large stems fresh coriander, chopped
1 litre (1³/4 pints) good-quality tomato juice
1 tablespoon Tabasco sauce
Salt and pepper
Extra vegetables and coriander leaves for garnish (optional)

1 Preheat the oven to 180°C/350°F/gas mark 4. Place the pepper halves cut side down on a baking tray and put in the oven for 20 minutes until the skins begin to wrinkle. Leave until cool enough to handle, then rub off the skins.

2 Put the other vegetables and the chopped coriander leaves into a food processor with 125ml (4fl oz) of the tomato juice. Whizz briefly so that the consistency is still quite rough.

3 Add the remaining juice and whizz at a low speed for 30 seconds. Pour into a jug and leave in the fridge until cold.

4 When ready to serve, add the Tabasco sauce and check and adjust seasoning.

5 Serve garnished with chopped tomato, peeled cucumber cubes, diced peppers, diced onion and coriander leave

ORAC value per serving ★

greens galore

This is one of my favourite soups, and I've made it here with baby spinach. The idea comes from the wonderful American cookery writer Patricia Wells, whose recipe for sorrel soup came from a German chef, as sorrel is widely grown there. I grow sorrel in my garden – it thrives like a weed – but it's quite difficult to find in most supermarkets in this country. What a shame! However, the soup can also be made with watercress, chard, dandelion leaves, young stinging nettles or a combination of all these healthy green leaves.

100g (3¹/2oz) baby spinach
50g (2oz) slightly softened unsalted butter
2 tablespoons extra-virgin olive oil
2 plump spring onions, sliced
175g (6oz) potatoes, peeled and diced
l litre (1³/4 pints) basic stock (see page 30)
250ml (9fl oz) double cream
12 chives, snipped
Salt and pepper

1 Put the washed spinach and butter into a food processor and whizz until puréed. Set aside in a cool place.

2 Heat the oil gently in a large saucepan, add the onions and sauté gently for 5 minutes.

3 Add the potatoes and cook gently, stirring occasionally, until the potatoes are coloured – about 10 minutes. Add the stock and simmer until the potatoes are tender.

5 Stir in the cream. Purée with a hand blender, or whizz in batches in the rinsed-out food processor.

6 If using a food processor, put the mixture back into the saucepan and check seasoning.

7 Whisk the spinach purée into the hot soup and scatter the chives on top.

ORAC value per serving ★★

mussel chowder

This recipe may look long, but it's very easy. I don't like mussels, but I love cooking this dish for friends; watching them enjoy it is reward enough for the small amount of trouble involved. It's full of essential fatty acids, rich in iodine and you don't need to worry about the double cream – it's only 50ml (2fl oz) per person, and enjoying good food is essential to good health. Add some good bread and a tomato and onion salad and you've got a complete meal and an extra ORAC *

1.5 kg (3lb 5oz) fresh mussels
1.5 litres (2¹/₂ pints) mixed dry white wine and basic stock
  (see page 30)
225g (8oz) potatoes, peeled and finely cubed
110g (4oz) unsalted butter
2 onions, finely chopped
2 garlic cloves, finely chopped
2 tablespoons flour
4 bay leaves
2 large sprigs thyme
200g (7oz) baby spinach
110g (4oz) defrosted frozen sweetcorn
12 large stems flat-leaf parsley
200ml (7fl oz) double cream

1 Wash the mussels, discarding any that are open, and pull off the beards. Put them in a large saucepan with the wine and stock.

2 Simmer for 10 minutes. Drain through a large sieve lined with kitchen muslin, reserving the cooking liquid. Discard any shells that still aren't open and remove the mussels from the rest.

3 Boil the potatoes in a separate saucepan for 10 minutes. Drain.

4 Meanwhile, melt the butter in a large saucepan. Add the onions and garlic and sauté gently for 5 minutes.

5 Stir in the flour and continue cooking, stirring continuously, for 2 minutes.

6 Pour in the wine and stock mixture, add the bay leaves and thyme, and simmer for 10 minutes.

7 Tear the spinach roughly and add to the pan with the sweetcorn, drained potatoes and mussels.

8 Reserve 8 parsley leaves and finely chop the rest. Add the chopped parsley to the pan and simmer gently for another 5 minutes.

9 Stir in the cream and heat through. Serve the chowder with the reserved parsley on top.

ORAC value per serving ★★★

tomato, pepper and pasta

This is another great one-pot meal – filling, full of vitamins and minerals, and an excellent source of ORAC units. If you can find them, the long, pointed, slightly misshapen peppers always seem to have more flavour.

4 tablespoons extra-virgin olive oil
1 red pepper, deseeded and cut into chunks
1 green pepper, deseeded and cut into chunks
1 yellow pepper, deseeded and cut into chunks
1 red onion, finely sliced
3 garlic cloves, finely chopped
1 tablespoon tomato purée
850ml (1½ pints) basic stock (see page 30)
2 large sprigs fresh rosemary
4 large sprigs thyme
400ml (14oz) canned chopped organic plum tomatoes
275g (10oz) pasta gnocchi – or the potato-based variety if you
    prefer
4 tablespoons freshly grated Parmesan cheese

1 Heat the oil in a large saucepan, add the peppers, onion and garlic, and gently sweat for 10 minutes, stirring regularly.

2 Mix in the tomato purée thoroughly.

3 Pour in the stock, add the thyme and rosemary as whole sprigs and bring to the boil.

4 Add the chopped tomatoes and simmer for 5 minutes.

5 Fish out the sprigs of herbs, put the soup into a food processor in batches, whizz until smooth and return to a clean saucepan.

6 Bring back to a simmer, add the gnocchi and heat for as long as instructed on the packet.

7 Serve the soup sprinkled with the Parmesan cheese

ORAC value per serving ★ノ

one-pot fish

This mixture of vegetables and fish produces a hearty stew-like soup that is rich in protein, vitamins and minerals, and contains very little fat. It's a perfect meal for anyone with heart problems, arthritis or any type of chest complaint.

To make your own fish stock, simmer fish trimmings with onion, fresh herbs and garlic. Some supermarket fishmongers will set the trimmings aside for you if you call a day in advance – and many reputable independent fishmongers do it as a matter of course.

1 parsnip, cubed
8 small new potatoes
50g (2oz) unsalted butter
1 sweet onion, very finely chopped
2 garlic cloves, very finely chopped
1 large or 2 small leeks, finely sliced
2 sticks celery, finely sliced
3 tablespoons flour
2 litres (3¹/2 pints) basic stock (see page 30) or, better still, home-made fish stock (see above)
About 500g (18oz) mixed cod, turbot, salmon, haddock or your favourites, cut into bite-sized chunks
8 large sprigs dill, chopped
¹/2 green cabbage, such as Savoy, very finely chopped
110g (4oz) frozen peas
3 pinches dried saffron
Freshly ground black pepper

1 Put the parsnip and potatoes into a saucepan of water and boil for 15 minutes until nearly tender.

2 Meanwhile, heat the butter in another saucepan and sauté the onion and garlic for 3 minutes.

3 Add the leeks and celery and continue cooking gently for another 3 minutes.

4 Stir in the flour, mix thoroughly and cook for 2 minutes.

5 Add the stock gradually, stirring continuously to ensure it remains smooth, and keep at simmering point.

6 Drain the parsnip and potatoes and add to the stock.

7 Season the fish fillets with the dill and black pepper, and set aside.

8 Add the cabbage to the pan with the peas and saffron, and continue to simmer for 5 minutes.

9 Add the fish and continue simmering for another 5 minutes until the fish is just tender.

ORAC value per serving ★★★★

chilled cherry

A favourite from eastern Europe, where luscious cherries grow in abundance. They're not only an extremely rich source of vitamin C, but also contain a group of naturally occurring chemicals called bioflavonoids, which protect the inner walls of your veins and arteries. The combination of cherries and prune juice gives this recipe an extremely high-ORAC score and the sweetness of the wine adds to the complexity of its taste.

800g (1³/4lb) fresh cherries (stoned weight)
200ml (7fl oz) prune juice
200ml (7fl oz) sweet white wine, such as Sauternes
3 tablespoons runny honey
2 tablespoons arrowroot

1 Put all but 4 of the cherries into a processor and whizz until smooth. Press firmly through a sieve to remove any skin and to extract the juices

2 Put the prune juice, white wine and honey into a saucepan. Heat gently until the honey is fully dissolved.

3 Add the cherry purée and heat gently.

4 Meanwhile, put the arrowroot into a small bowl and mix in just enough water to make a thick, smooth paste. Mix it into the soup and continue heating very gently until the soup starts to thicken. Remove from the heat, leave to cool, then put into the fridge to chill.

5 Halve the remaining 4 cherries, float on the soup, and serve.

ORAC value per serving ★★★

easy tomato

Home-made tomato soup in less than 30 minutes – what could be easier? It not only tastes good, but the essential oils in the basil are powerfully mood enhancing, so it makes you feel good, too. Not surprisingly, this recipe also does you good, as it's super-rich in betacarotenes and cancer-preventive lycopene and has a high-ORAC score as well.

3 tablespoons olive oil
1 onion, finely sliced
3 garlic cloves, chopped
2 young celery sticks, finely sliced
2 tablespoons sun-dried tomato purée
700ml (1¹/4 pints) basic stock (see page 30)
275g (10oz) roasted peppers, drained and sliced if necessary
1 large sprig rosemary
800g (1³/4lb) canned organic whole plum tomatoes
12 basil leaves
Salt and pepper

1 Heat the oil in a saucepan, add the onion and garlic, and sauté gently until soft – about 5 minutes.

2 Add the celery and continue cooking for another 5 minutes.

3 Stir in the sun-dried tomato purée and combine thoroughly.

4 Add the stock, peppers, rosemary and tomatoes with their juices, and simmer gently for 15 minutes.

5 Fish out the rosemary, adjust the seasoning and serve with the whole basil leaves scattered on top.

ORAC value per serving ★✶

real chicken

Thanks to the special amino acids in chicken soup, this really does have a penicillin-like effect. Of course it's delicious at any time, but for the sick or convalescing it does have immune-boosting properties. It's not particularly high in ORAC value, but when combined with the other benefits, this is a double-whammy recipe.

1 left-over carcass of a cooked chicken
1 large onion, unpeeled and quartered
3 bay leaves
6 whole peppercorns
1 bouquet garni
2 large carrots, diced
1/2 swede, diced
1 parsnip, diced
2 small turnips, diced
1 sweet potato, peeled and diced
Salt and freshly ground black pepper

1 Put the chicken carcass into a large saucepan and cover with about 1.2 litres (2 pints) of water.

2 Add the onion, bay leaves, peppercorns and bouquet garni to the pan, bring to the boil and simmer, covered, for 2 hours. Strain and return the broth to the pan.

3 Add the carrot, swede, parsnip, turnip and sweet potato to the broth, bring back to the boil and simmer until the vegetables are tender – about 30 minutes.

4 4 Season to taste.

ORAC value per serving ★★

cream of broccoli and brussels sprouts

This is one sure way to get youngsters to eat Brussels sprouts and broccoli, although it's probably best to omit the almonds for young children just in case of allergies. This is an immensely cancer-protective soup as these vegetables are exceptionally rich in anti-cancer plant chemicals. Not surpisingly, the ORAC score is quite high.

3 tablespoons extra-virgin olive oil
1 onion, finely chopped
1.2 litres (2 pints) basic stock (see page 30)
2 broccoli heads cut into florets
350g (12oz) Brussels sprouts, halved
1 bouquet garni
110g (4oz) ground almonds
300ml (1/2 pint) single cream
4 tablespoons slivered almonds

1 Heat the oil in a large saucepan. Add the onion and sweat gently for 5 minutes. Add the stock and bring to the boil.

2 Add the broccoli, Brussels sprouts, bouquet garni and ground almonds. Simmer gently until the vegetables are just tender, 10–15 minutes.

3 Fish out the bouquet garni and liquidise the soup, in batches, in a food processor. Return to the pan.

4 Stir in the cream and heat through. Serve with the slivered almonds floating on top.

ORAC value per serving ★↗

black bean

My first taste of this soup was on a hot, humid night in the middle of the rainy season chugging up the Amazon in a small boat. The Brazilian woman doing the cooking was a magician with beans – a staple food in that part of South America. She used far more chillies and garlic than I do in this recipe, but, surprisingly, the intense sweating that her thick dish of soup produced was quite cooling in the tropical heat. If you can't find black beans, it works just as well with haricot, flageolet or borlotti beans – but it doesn't look quite as dramatic.

150g (5oz) dried black beans
1.5 litres (2¹/₂ pints) basic stock (see page 30) or chicken stock
from the chicken soup recipe (see page 40)
12 stems savory
4 bay leaves
4 tablespoons rapeseed oil
1 large onion, finely sliced
4 garlic cloves, finely sliced
3 red chillies, deseeded and chopped
400g (14oz) canned organic tomatoes, coarsely chopped

1 Rinse the beans thoroughly. If using black beans, put into a saucepan of cold water, bring to the boil and boil for 10 minutes. Drain.

2 Rinse the saucepan, return the beans and add the stock, savory and bay leaves. Cover and simmer until tender – this could take a couple of hours. Add extra stock or water if too much of the liquid evaporates.

3 Heat the oil in a deep frying pan and sweat the onion, garlic and chillies for 5 minutes.

4 Add the tomatoes and continue cooking, stirring well, until combined.

5 Stir the contents of this pan into the beans and stock. Simmer for 5 minutes, then strain, reserving the stock. Remove the bay leaves.

6 Liquidise the beans and vegetables, in batches if necessary, with a ladleful of stock.

7 Return all the puréed vegetables and stock to a clean pan, stir and heat through.

ORAC value per serving ★★★★

cabbage and beetroot

Throughout Europe, cabbage is known as the medicine of the poor – and with good reason. It's rich in vitamin C and antibacterial sulphur as well as containing large amounts of cancer-protective plant chemicals. Beetroot is a seriously under-valued vegetable, which is excellent for blood conditions like anaemia and is traditionally given to people with leukaemia in Eastern Europe. This peasant soup from Poland looks beautiful, tastes delicious and will do you more good than a bottle of vitamin pills.

4 tablespoons rapeseed oil
1 onion, finely chopped
1 garlic clove, finely chopped
450g (1lb) raw baby beetroot, diced
1 litre (1³/4 pints) basic stock (see page 30)
2 tablespoons cider vinegar
275g (10oz) white cabbage, coarsely shredded
8 chives

1 Heat the oil in a large saucepan, add the onion and garlic, and sweat gently for 5 minutes.

2 Mix in the beetroot, pour in the stock and boil until tender. Whizz in a blender with the cider vinegar and return to the saucepan.

3 Scatter the cabbage on the soup, but don't stir. Cover and boil gently for 5 minutes, until the cabbage is almost cooked but still crunchy.

4 Serve with chives arranged on top.

salads

All recipes in this chapter serve 4 unless otherwise stated

ORAC value per serving ★★

beetroot, pink grapefruit and red onion

The eye appeal of these wonderful colours is enough to make you feel good before you even taste this dish. But when you add the blood benefits of beetroot, the heart-protective qualities from the grapefruit and the disease-fighting chemicals in onions, you really have good health on a plate.

4 small, cooked beetroot, sliced
2 pink grapefruit, peeled and divided into segments
2 red onions, sliced
1 quantity creamy yogurt dressing (see page 133)

1 Arrange the salad ingredients alternately around the sides of 4 plates or in a salad bowl.

2 Pour the dressing on top.

ORAC value per serving ★

roasted beetroot on a bed of red lettuce

This recipe brings out all the flavours of beetroot, enhanced with the antibacterial, antiviral and antifungal properties of garlic and the spicy taste of mustard and good olive oil.

8 baby beetroot, trimmed and rinsed, keeping skins intact
75g (3oz) unsalted butter
4 tablespoons extra-virgin olive oil
2 large spring onions, finely chopped
Juice of 1 lime
2 garlic cloves, finely chopped
1/2 teaspoon dry mustard
1 large head radicchio or other red lettuce

1 Preheat the oven to 200°C/400°F/gas mark 6.

2 Cut 8 pieces of kitchen foil large enough to envelop the beetroot and rub each piece with butter. Wrap 1 piece of foil around each beetroot. Place the beetroots in the oven and bake for about 1 hour and 15 minutes.

3 Meanwhile, make the dressing. Put the olive oil in a mixing bowl. Add the onion, lime juice, garlic and mustard and whisk well. Set aside to let the flavours intermingle.

4 When the beetroots are cool enough to handle, but still warm, remove from foil, rub off the skins and slice.

5 Arrange the lettuce leaves on 4 plates, lay the beetroot slices on top and drizzle with the dressing.

ORAC value per serving ★★

middle eastern couscous salad

Cooking the couscous in home-made stock immediately adds to the ORAC score of this salad. Including the cleansing properties of asparagus and the huge betacarotene content of sun-dried tomatoes with the medicinal benefits of the fresh herbs results in a highly nutritious salad with an excellent ORAC score.

110g (4oz) couscous
450ml (16fl oz) basic stock (see page 30) or stock from the
  chicken soup (see page 40)
175g (6oz) sun-dried tomatoes, chopped
4 tablespoons extra-virgin olive oil
1 courgette, diced
1 red pepper, deseeded and diced
12 fresh asparagus tips
4 tablespoons mixed soft herbs, such as flat-leaf parsley, tarragon,
  chervil and oregano, finely chopped
2 large tomatoes, sliced

1 Put the couscous into a large saucepan with the stock and cook according to packet instructions.

2 Meanwhile, soak the sun-dried tomatoes in freshly boiled water for 2 minutes and snip into 1cm (1/2in) strips.

3 Heat the oil in a frying pan and gently sauté the courgette, pepper, asparagus and tomatoes for 5 minutes.

4 Tip the couscous into a bowl and mix in the sautéd vegetables.

5 Stir the herbs into the couscous and top with the sliced tomatoes.

ORAC value per serving ★✦

wild and red rice on radicchio

The wonderful red colour in the Camargue rice contrasts beautifully with the blackness of wild rice. And serving each portion inside a whole head of radicchio is certainly eye-catching. The dried apricots, cherries and raisins provide instant energy from their fruit sugars, as well as essential minerals and plently of fibre.

110g (4oz) Camargue rice
110g (4oz) wild rice
4 small heads radicchio, trimmed and thoroughly washed
50g (2oz) dried cherries, snipped
75g (3oz) no-need-to-soak dried apricots, snipped
50g (2oz) raisins
50g (2oz) chopped walnuts
1 quantity standard French dressing (see page 132)

1 Cook the two rices in separate saucepans, following the packet instructions. Drain if necessary and leave to cool.

2 Meanwhile, open the crowns of the radicchio carefully.

3 Mix the cherries and apricots with the raisins and walnuts.

4 Mix the rices together. Tip in the fruits and nuts, and stir until combined.

5 Pour on the dressing and stir thoroughly.

6 Put the rice, fruit and nut mixture into the centre of the radicchio.

ORAC value per serving ★

traditional salade niçoise

This is the ubiquitous recipe from the South of France, and is ideal reminiscence therapy. If you've ever eaten it under the Mediterranean sun, you need only one sniff of its distinctive aroma to transport you back to the pavement café and happy memories. Lots of essential fatty acids and bone-building vitamin D from the fish, carbohydrate, protein, vitamins A and C, iron and other minerals from the rest of the ingredients make this a complete meal.

225g (8oz) Jersey new potatoes
4 organic free-range eggs
175g (6oz) French beans, trimmed
1 large cos lettuce
150g (5oz) canned tuna, drained
½ cucumber, peeled, deseeded and cut into julienne strips
4 plum tomatoes, coarsely chopped
100g (3½oz) canned or bottled anchovies, drained
10 stoned black olives, halved
½ quantity standard French dressing (see page 132)

1 Scrub the potatoes and boil until tender. Halve and leave to cool.

2 Semi hard-boil the eggs for 6 minutes and rinse under cold running water to prevent discolouring. Peel and quarter when they're cool enough to handle.

3 Simmer the beans until just tender, let cool, then cut into 2.5cm (1in) sticks.

4 Separate the lettuce leaves and lay in a large bowl. Pile on the potatoes and beans.

5 Flake the tuna and arrange on the beans. Add the cucumber, tomatoes and quartered eggs. Arrange the anchovies on top of the eggs.

6 Scatter the olives on top, and pour on the dressing.

oracle timbale

A substantial salad that combines the crunchy sweetness of carrot, the heat of the radish and the unmistakable celery flavour of celeriac. Extra iron from the raisins and the blood-building red pigments in beetroot make this good to eat at any time, but especially useful if you're recovering from an illness or operation.

1 large carrot, trimmed, peeled and grated
1 mouli (white radish), trimmed, peeled and grated
1/2 celeriac, trimmed, peeled and grated
2 beetroots, trimmed, peeled and grated
400g (14oz) cooked basmati rice
2 tablespoons finely chopped flat-leaf parsley
1 tablespoon finely snipped chives
110g (4oz) raisins
2 tablespoons extra-virgin olive oil
8 whole chives

1 Mix the grated vegetables thoroughly with the cooked rice.

2 Add the parsley, snipped chives, raisins and olive oil and stir again.

3 Firmly press the mixture into 4 timbale pots and refrigerate for at least 1 hour before turning out.

4 Decorate with the whole chives.

ORAC value per serving ★★★

warm chicken livers with berries

Now that nobody gets their chicken liver inside the bird, you can buy them in packs in virtually any supermarket. You may have to look further for organic livers, but it's worth the effort. As well as massive amounts of vitamins A and B12, you'll get plenty of iron, lots of vitamin C and a high-ORAC score.

400g (14oz) organic chicken livers
2 tablespoons olive oil
25g (1oz) unsalted butter
1 large sprig rosemary
2 garlic cloves, finely chopped
1/2 head cos lettuce
1/2 head red frisée
3 large spring onions, finely chopped
12 cherry tomatoes, halved
150g (5oz) mixed blackberries and blueberries
1/2 quantity standard French dressing (see page 132)

1 Wash the chicken livers and snip off any pieces of fat or membrane.

2 Heat the oil and butter in a frying pan and sauté the livers in them, with the rosemary and garlic, until cooked but still soft – this should take about 5 minutes. Remove the rosemary.

3 Meanwhile, separate the lettuce and frisée leaves and put into a large salad bowl. Mix in the spring onions.

4 Put the tomatoes around the sides of the lettuce. Spoon the chicken livers into the middle, reserving the cooking juices, and scatter the blueberries and blackberries on top.

5 Put the salad dressing into a cold jug. Add the reserved cooking juices and mix well. Pour over the salad and serve.

ORAC value per serving ★✦

tabbouleh with a difference

The mixture of bulgar wheat, cucumber and mint is what gives this dish its distinctly Middle Eastern flavour. But it's the blueberries that account for its high ORAC score. This salad also provides large amounts of vitamin C well in excess of your daily requirement.

110g (4oz) bulgar wheat
1 cucumber, peeled, deseeded and diced
1 large red onion, very finely chopped
4 large tomatoes, coarsely chopped
6 large sprigs each mint and parsley, roughly chopped
150g (5oz) blueberries
1/2 quantity standard French dressing (see page 132)

1 Put the bulgar wheat into a bowl, cover with cold water and leave until swollen – about 30 minutes.

2 Drain the bulgar. Mix in the cucumber, onion, tomatoes, mint and parsley. Scatter the blueberries on top and pour on the dressing.

ORAC value per serving ★★

kiwi fruit, berries and cottage cheese

Contrary to popular perception, the kiwi fruit is not just a decorative addition to your cooking. In fact, it's extremely rich in vitamin C – far more per 100g than oranges – and is also a good source of fibre, betacarotene and vitamin E. In this dish, the unusual combination of strawberries and balsamic vinegar results in a surprising and interesting flavour, enhanced by the high-ORAC scores of the blueberries and green pepper.

4 large kiwi fruit, peeled and sliced widthways
8 large strawberries, sliced lengthways
350g (12oz) cottage cheese
1 large green pepper, deseeded and finely cubed
110g (4oz) blueberries
6 large sprigs mint, finely chopped
100ml (3¹/2fl oz) extra-virgin olive oil
30ml (1fl oz) organic balsamic vinegar
1 teaspoon Dijon mustard
Coarsely ground black pepper

1 Arrange the kiwi fruit and strawberries alternately around the rims of 4 small plates,

2 Mix the green pepper with the cottage cheese and season well with coarsely ground black pepper.

3 Put a mound of the cottage cheese mixture in the middle of each plate and scatter the blueberries on top.

4 Sprinkle the mint over the blueberries.

5 Mix the oil, vinegar and mustard together, and pour over the cottage cheese.

ORAC value per serving ★★★★

watercress, chicory and alfalfa

Like all sprouted seeds, alfalfa sprouts are a rich source of nutrients, designed by nature to provide everything the growing plant needs. With all the cancer-protective chemicals in watercress, the natural sugars in grapes and plenty of vitamin C, this is a maximum-vitality dish with an enormous ORAC score.

2 large bunches or bags watercress, about 300g (11oz)
3 heads chicory
1 large, sweet Spanish onion, finely chopped
400g (14oz) seedless black grapes, halved
450g (1lb) alfalfa sprouts (or bean sprouts), washed and drained
1 quantity creamy yogurt dressing (see page 133)

1 Wash and pick over the watercress, and separate the chicory heads into separate leaves.

2 Place the watercress and chicory in a bowl, add the onion, grapes and alfalfa (or bean) sprouts, and mix.

3 Pour on the dressing and mix again.

red, red, red

Trust the French to come up with the idea of eating radishes smeared with butter and dipped in coarse sea salt – delicious, but hardly a treat for your heart and blood pressure. Here, the fabulous health properties of the radish, which, together with garlic and onions, was used by the ancient pharaohs to pay workers building the pyramids, gives the bite to this high-ORAC salad.

1 largish head radicchio
1 large red pepper, deseeded and finely diced
175g (6oz) radishes, sliced
4 small, cooked beetroot, diced
1 small red onion, finely sliced
225g (8oz) frozen cranberries, defrosted – better still, fresh,
*   if you can get them*
1 quantity creamy yogurt dressing (see page 133)
10 young sprigs chervil

1 Arrange a nest of radicchio leaves in a large bowl.

2 Mix together the red pepper, radishes, beetroot and onion, and put into the radicchio nest.

3 Mix the cranberries gently into the dressing and pour over the salad.

4 Serve with the whole chervil sprigs scattered on top.

sweet and peppery

Mixing the sweetness of raspberries and watermelon with the hot peppery taste of watercress and the mild flavour of red onion is what gives this salad its unique 'fusion' appeal. I first ate watercress and onion as a salad in a beach café overlooking the Indian Ocean on the island of Mauritius, where, strangely, watercress is the favourite salad ingredient.

1 large bunch or bag watercress, about 150g (5oz)
1/2 watermelon, deseeded and cut into bite-sized cubes
1 large red onion, very finely chopped
250g (9oz) raspberries
250ml (9fl oz) organic, unfiltered apple juice
Coarsely ground black pepper

1 Pick over the watercress and put into a salad bowl. Add the watermelon and onion, and mix.

2 Scatter the raspberries on top.

3 Pour on the apple juice and top with lots of coarsely ground black pepper.

ORAC value per serving ★★

green and red fusilli

Like all pasta salads, this one is substantial enough to be a meal on its own. Energy-giving carbohydrates, protein, calcium, masses of betacarotene and cholesterol-lowering monounsaturated fat from the olive oil also make this extremely healthy, with an excellent ORAC score.

400g (14oz) mixed tomato and spinach fusilli
Florets of1 large head broccoli, very large ones halved
150g (5oz) baby spinach
1 red onion, very finely chopped
200g (7oz) seedless black grapes, halved
125ml (4fl oz) extra-virgin olive oil
3 tablespoons freshly grated Parmesan cheese

1 Cook the pasta according to the packet instructions. Drain and put into a large, warm bowl.

2 Meanwhile, plunge the broccoli into a saucepan of fast boiling water for 5 minutes.

3 Wash the spinach, leaving any water still clinging to the leaves. Place in another pan, cover and cook until wilted – this should take 3–5 minutes, depending on the age of the leaves.

4 Drain the green vegetables and tip them into the pasta with the onion and grapes. Stir gently but thoroughly, being careful not to break up the broccoli florets.

5 Pour the olive oil over the mixture, add the Parmesan, mix gently again and serve.

ORAC value per serving ★★

beans bonus

All beans are a healthy addition to the diet, as they contain protein, carbohydrate, vitamins, minerals and fibre, with the bonus of phyto-oestrogens. It's these natural plant hormones that are so important for women, as they help prevent osteoporosis and control the unpleasant side-effects of the menopause. Combining broad beans and chickpeas with all the other ingredients provides a generous helping of essential nutrients and a high-ORAC score.

500g (18oz) shelled baby broad beans – frozen are fine if you
   can't find fresh
225g (8oz) canned or cooked chickpeas, rinsed and drained
50g (2oz) sun-dried tomatoes, snipped into slithers
3 large spring onions, finely chopped
1 bulb fennel, trimmed and sliced lengthways
Leaves of 3 sprigs fresh thyme
3 stalks sage, finely chopped
4 stalks flat-leaf parsley, finely chopped
4 large plum tomatoes, coarsely chopped
1 quantity creamy yogurt dressing (see page 133)

1 Cook the broad beans and pinch them to remove the skins. This isn't strictly necessary and it is rather time-consuming, but it does make a difference to both the look and flavour of the dish.

2 Put the beans into a large salad bowl. Add the chickpeas, sun-dried tomatoes, spring onions, fennel, thyme, sage and fresh tomatoes, and mix thoroughly.

3 Pour on the salad dressing and mix again.

ORAC value per serving ★★★

mediterranean mix

Here's another recipe redolent of hot summer days and balmy evenings on the beach anywhere in the Mediterranean. Wonderful ripe tomatoes, succulent and flavoursome sweet peppers and the coolness of cucumber add up to a feast of vitamins and a super-protective anti-ageing ORAC score.

350g (12oz) frozen sweetcorn
1 red pepper, deseeded and finely diced
1 yellow pepper, deseeded and finely diced
1 cucumber, peeled, deseeded and diced
150g (5oz) radishes, sliced
1 sweet Spanish onion, finely chopped
5 plum tomatoes, finely chopped and juices retained
110g (4oz) raisins
1 quantity standard French dressing (see page 132)

1 Cook the sweetcorn and leave to cool.

2 Put into a bowl with the peppers, cucumber, radishes, onion, tomatoes and raisins.

3 Pour the dressing on top and mix gently.

light meals

All recipes in this chapter serve 4 unless otherwise stated

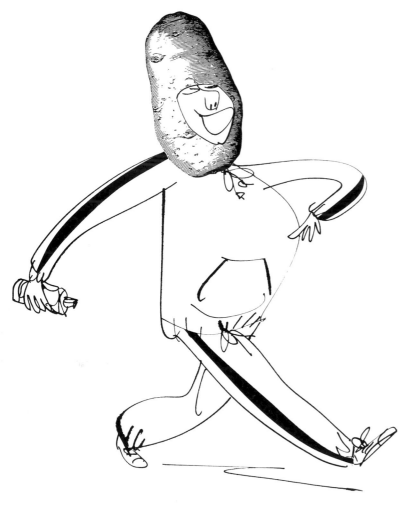

ORAC value per serving ★★

spanish omelette

Equally good to eat hot or cold, this is a satisfying and substantial light meal. It's extremely rich in vitamin C and has lots of good carbohydrates, iron, B vitamins and proteins from the eggs, and all the protective natural chemicals from the onion.

350g (12oz) frozen peas
5 tablespoons olive oil
200g (7oz) potatoes, peeled and diced
1 large onion, roughly chopped
2 red peppers, deseeded and cubed
12 free-range organic eggs, well beaten
Salt and pepper

1 Place the peas in a saucepan of water, boil for 3 minutes, then drain.

2 Heat the oil in a very large frying pan – or 2 small ones (if you're cooking in batches, divide the ingredient amounts between the pans).

3 Add the potatoes and stir until just turning golden.

4 Add the onions and peppers, and cook until soft.

5 Stir in the peas.

6 Season the eggs, pour into the pan and leave until the edges start to firm. Gently tip the pan to distribute the eggs evenly. When the base is firm but the top still runny, put under a hot grill to finish cooking.

ORAC value per serving ★★★

broccoli and cauliflower cheese

Either a complete light meal for 4 or an excellent vegetable dish with a main course, comfortably serving 6 to 8 people. The cancer-protective properties of broccoli and cauliflower are well documented, and the lycopene from the dried and fresh tomatoes adds a huge prostate-protective boost for men and helps reduce the risk of breast cancer for women.

1 large cauliflower, separated into florets
2 large heads broccoli, separated into florets
200g (7oz) bottled sun-dried tomatoes, drained and halved
50g (2oz) unsalted butter
2 tablespoons flour
700ml (1¼ pints) semi-skimmed milk
200g (7oz) strong Cheddar cheese, grated
4 large plum tomatoes, sliced
2 tablespoons freshly grated Parmesan cheese

1 Preheat the oven to 220°C/425°F/gas mark 7. Place the cauliflower and broccoli florets into a pan of boiling water. Cook for 5 minutes, drain and refresh under cold water.

2 Arrange alternate florets in rows in a flat casserole dish and scatter the sun-dried tomatoes on top.

3 Heat the butter gently in a large frying pan. When melted, stir in the flour and cook for 2 minutes, stirring constantly, until the mixture thickens.

4 Gradually add the milk, again stirring continuously, and continue cooking until it forms a sauce. Add the grated cheese and stir until it's completely melted. Pour the sauce over the vegetables and arrange the tomatoes on top.

7 Sprinkle with the Parmesan, place in the oven and bake for 20 minutes, until the sauce is bubbling.

ORAC value per serving ★★★

vegetable risotto

Don't even think about risotto if you haven't got arborio rice, as no other variety works as well. The combination of peas, asparagus and baby spinach is what gives this creamy, light risotto such a good ORAC score, with the bonus of extra calcium from the mascarpone.

3 tablespoons olive oil
4 plump spring onions, cut into large chunks
225g (8oz) arborio rice
150g (5oz) frozen peas
12 asparagus tips
900ml (1¾ pints) basic stock (see page 30)
110g (4oz) baby spinach or rocket
3 tablespoons mascarpone cheese

1 Heat the oil in a large saucepan, add the onions and sauté gently for 2 minutes. Add the rice and stir for 1 minute.

2 Mix in the peas and asparagus tips, and add enough stock just to cover. Stir until the stock is almost absorbed. Continue gradually adding stock and stirring gently, without breaking up the asparagus tips, until the rice is tender.

3 Add the spinach or rocket and stir for 1 minute. Remove from the heat, stir in the mascarpone cheese and serve.

ORAC value per serving ★★★

guacamole and salad

I've never understood why most people – and especially women – worry about avocados being fattening. They avoid them like the plague, put sweeteners and skimmed milk in their coffee and then eat a Danish pastry! Avocados contain monounsaturated fats, which are heart-protective and help the body get rid of cholesterol. They're also extremely rich in vitamin E, which is known to protect against some forms of cancer and helps prevent heart and circulatory disease. This delicious light meal has an extremely high-ORAC score.

2 large ripe avocados
Juice of 2 lemons
2 garlic cloves, finely chopped
2 large tomatoes, chopped
5 tablespoons natural, organic bio-yogurt
1 teaspoon Worcester sauce
1 large red onion, sliced
2 large tomatoes, sliced
300g (11oz) alfalfa sprouts
1 quantity standard French dressing (see page 132)
8 wholemeal pitta breads

1 Peel the avocados and mash the flesh roughly.

2 Put into a bowl with the lemon juice, garlic, chopped tomatoes, yogurt and Worcester sauce, and mix thoroughly. Place in fridge.

3 Place the tomato slices, onion and alfalfa sprouts in a salad bowl, pour on the dressing and mix.

4 Warm the pitta bread, cut each one in 4 widthways and serve with the guacamole dip and salad.

ORAC value per serving ★★

pickled herring with potato and tomato salad

A variation of this popular Scandinavian dish, which adds to the essential oil and vitamin D in the herrings a huge amount of lycopene and a good ORAC score from the tomatoes.

350g (12oz) new potatoes, such as Charlotte
4 rollmop herrings
110g (4oz) sun-dried tomatoes, cubed
4 tablespoons extra-virgin olive oil

1 Scrub the potatoes, but don't peel them. Place in a saucepan of water, bring to the boil and cook until just tender. Leave to cool slightly.

2 Unwrap the rollmops, keeping all the onion inside, and place each one on a plate.

3 Quarter the potatoes and mix with the tomatoes. Drizzle with the olive oil.

4 Serve the potato and tomato mixture alongside the herrings.

ORAC value per serving ★★★

stuffed red peppers

Wonderful to eat hot or cold, but I love them just warm in the Italian style. Red peppers are a nutritional feast on their own, and when you add the valuable antioxidants in sweetcorn and the unique lung-cancer protective chemicals in watercress, you have an ORAC feast as well.

110g (4oz) rice
2 tablespoons extra-virgin olive oil
I large onion, finely chopped
200g (7oz) frozen sweetcorn
Leaves of 1 bunch or bag watercress, about 100g (3¹/₂oz)
4 large red peppers – choose squat vegetables with flat bottoms, as they have to stand up during cook
8 tablespoons freshly grated Parmesan cheese
1 quantity hot tomato salsa (see page 123)

1 Preheat the oven to180°C/350°F/gas mark 4.

2 Cook the rice according to instructions on the packet.

3 Heat the oil in a deep frying pan or saucepan, add the onion and sauté gently until soft – about 5 minutes.

4 Drain the cooked rice, pour into the onion and stir until coated with the oil. Add the sweetcorn and mix thoroughly.

5 Add the watercress leaves and mix again.

6 Cut the red peppers in half widthways, trim the stalk until that end can sit upright, remove the seeds and thick membrane. Soak the peppers in boiling water for 5 minutes.

7 Drain and stand the halved peppers in a large baking or casserole dish, and spoon the rice mixture into each cavity. Add 5 tablespoons of water to the dish, cover with foil and bake for 30 minutes.

8 Remove the foil, sprinkle on the Parmesan cheese and bake for 10 minutes.

9 Serve with the hot tomato salsa on the side.

ORAC value per serving ★★⌐

vegetable stir-fry

Epidemiologists, scientists who study the health of different populations, have long known about the health benefits of the way people in the Far East eat. There, the most common cooking utensil is the wok, and stir-frying is one of the best ways of conserving the nutrient content of vegetables, cooking them very quickly and maintaining their colour and flavour. This is real fast food, with a healthy ORAC bonus.

3 tablespoons rapeseed oil – preferably organic, but certainly GM-free
3 carrots cut into 2.5cm (1in) julienne strips
110g (4oz) fine French beans, trimmed and halved
200g (7oz) frozen sweetcorn, thawed
3 heads pak choi, trimmed, cut into 6 lengthways, woody parts removed
350g (12oz) mixed fresh alfalfa sprouts and bean sprouts – ideally, use equal amounts, but if you can't find alfalfa, bean sprouts alone will do
1 quantity fresh tomato sauce (see page 122)
2 tablespoons light soy sauce

1 Heat the oil in a wok or very large frying pan, tip in the carrots and beans, and stir-fry for 2 minutes.

2 Add the sweetcorn and pak choi, and continue to stir-fry for 1 minute or until the pak choi is just wilted.

3 Add the alfalfa and bean sprouts and cook for 1–2 minutes, until cooked but still crunchy.

4 Pour in the tomato sauce and soy sauce, reduce heat slightly and stir until heated through – about 3 minutes.

ORAC value per serving ★⌐

tofu and honey treat

In parts of the world where soy-based foods are eaten regularly there's only a fraction of the osteoporosis that we suffer in the West, and women going through the menopause are spared most of the unpleasant symptoms, especially the hot flushes. The reason is that they eat far more natural plant oestrogens, which are here in abundance, thanks to the tofu. Adding the monounsaturated oil and minerals in walnuts, with the benefits of beans, cranberries and garlic, makes this a tasty and crunchy light meal.

1 garlic clove, finely chopped
1 tablespoon runny honey
1 teaspoon Tabasco sauce
1 tablespoon light soy sauce
250g (9oz) tofu, diced
225g (8oz) green beans, mange tout or sugar snap peas
110g (4oz) fresh or frozen cranberries, thawed
3 tablespoons rapeseed oil
75g (3oz) chopped walnuts

1 Mix together the garlic, honey, Tabasco and soy sauce. Pour over the tofu and place in the fridge for 1 hour.

2 Meanwhile, cook the beans or peas – about 15 minutes.

3 If you haven't had time to defrost the frozen cranberries, soak in enough boiling water just to cover and leave for 10 minutes.

4 Heat the oil in a large frying pan. Add cranberries, walnuts and drained tofu, and cook gently, stirring constantly, for 2 minutes. Add the tofu marinade, mix in beans or peas and heat through.

tuna and bean salad

As well as having a good ORAC score, this quick and simple dish provides essential fatty acids and vitamin D from the tuna, lots of vital vitamins and minerals and a huge amount of soluble fibre to help control cholesterol and improve digestion.

4 free-range organic eggs
220g (8oz) canned kidney beans, rinsed and drained
220g (8oz) canned borlotti beans, rinsed and drained
220g (8oz) canned flageolet beans, rinsed and drained
200g (7oz) canned sweetcorn, rinsed and drained
400g (14oz) canned tuna – preferably in spring water–drained
1 large red onion, chopped
2 large carrots, grated
1 red pepper, deseeded and cubed
3 large handfuls rocket (or baby spinach), thick stems removed
6 tablespoons standard French dressing (see page 132)

1 Semi hard-boil the eggs: put into cold water, bring to a simmer and cook for 6 minutes. Shell the eggs and cut into quarters.

2 Put the drained beans, sweetcorn and tuna into a large bowl. Mix in the onion, carrot and rocket (or spinach). Pour on the dressing and toss the salad to mix.

3 Serve with the eggs on top.

sweetcorn, sweet potato and beetroot fritters

These fritters can be eaten hot or cold with a salad as a light meal, but they also make an excellent accompaniment floating on top of soups or used as a base on which to serve other savoury dishes. The horseradish and beetroot sauce adds an unusual hot, sweet flavour as well as boosting the ORAC score.

200g (7oz) frozen sweetcorn, thawed
2 large sweet potatoes, peeled and grated
4 beetroots, cooked (but not pickled) and grated
2 tablespoons flour
2 free-range organic eggs, beaten
Rapeseed oil
Horseradish and beetroot sauce (see page 125)

1 Mix the sweetcorn, potatoes and beetroot together in a bowl.

2 Whisk the flour into the eggs and mix into the vegetables.

3 Form the vegetable mixture into 8 equal portions and flatten.

4 Pour enough oil into a frying pan to cover it to a depth of about 5mm (1/4in). Fry the fritters for about 3 minutes on each side.

5 Serve with horseradish and beetroot sauce and a green salad.

ORAC value per serving ★★★✦

tofu and noodle stir-fry

Super healthy though it may be, even its most dedicated fans would have to admit that tofu equals tasteless. Happily, it's brilliant at absorbing flavours, and marinating it in this fantastic mixture of lime, mango, Tabasco and garlic results in a piquant taste. This is a very high ORAC dish, with the bonus of one of the most cancer-protective of all the cabbage family, kale.

Juice of 1 lime
1 large mango, peeled, stoned and chopped
1/2 teaspoon Tabasco
2 garlic cloves, finely chopped
250g (8oz) tofu, cubed
4 tablespoons sesame oil
1 onion, chopped
75g (3oz) instant noodles
110g (4oz) kale, finely shredded
275g (10oz) alfalfa sprouts (or bean sprouts)

1 Preheat the oven to 220°C/425°F/gas mark 7.

2 Mix the lime juice, mango, Tabasco and half the garlic in a large ovenproof dish. Add the tofu, stir to coat in the marinade and set aside for 30 minutes.

3 Place the tofu in its marinade in the oven and bake for 20 minutes.

4 Meanwhile, heat the oil in a wok or large frying pan. Add the onion and remaining garlic and soften for 5 minutes.

5 In a saucepan, cook the noodles according to packet instructions – usually around 2 minutes.

6 Add the kale to the onions and garlic and cook, stirring continuously, until wilted.

7 Still stirring, add the alfalfa sprouts and cook until transparent.

8 Drain the noodles, add to the vegetables, and cook for a further 2 minutes.

9 Remove the tofu from the oven, add to the vegetables with the marinade, stir, and serve.

ORAC value per serving ★★

sardine and tomato pâté with watercress salad

There's no doubt that, generally speaking, fresh food is best. But there are three exceptions – canned sardines being one. (Tomatoes and beans are the other two: tomatoes for their higher lycopene content and beans for their convenience.) Superior to any bought fish pâté, this dish has bone-building calcium and vitamin D, lung-protective watercress and a good ORAC score.

230g (8oz) canned sardines, drained
3 tablespoons tomato purée
1 tablespoon horseradish sauce (see page 124)
75g (3oz) unsalted butter
8 plum tomatoes, halved lengthways
8 spring onions, trimmed and shredded lengthways
1 bag or bunch watercress, about 100g (3¹/₂oz), woody stems removed

1 Mash the sardines and stir in the tomato purée and horseradish.

2 Melt the butter, being careful not to burn it. Add half to the fish mixture and mix well.

3 Transfer the mixture to a terrine or other suitable container.

4 Push the plum tomatoes into the surface of the fish, cut side up, pour the rest of the butter over the top, and leave to chill in the fridge for at least 1 hour.

5 Mix the spring onions and watercress together in a bowl. Add the French dressing and toss.

6 Remove the terrine from the fridge, slice and serve with salad.

ORAC value per serving ★★★

prawn couscous with raisins

The mixture of couscous, raisins and prawns with the spicy fish dressing provides the distinctive Middle Eastern flavour of this recipe. Quick and simple, this makes a delicious light meal for 4 or a starter for 6. As well as betacarotene, vitamins A and C, iron and plenty of fibre from the other ingredients, you'll get a valuable ORAC score

175g (6oz) raisins
350g (12oz) couscous
About 500ml (16fl oz) basic stock (see page 30)
225g (8oz) cooked, peeled prawns
¹/₂ large cucumber, peeled, deseeded and cubed
1 red pepper, deseeded and cubed
1 green pepper, deseeded and cubed
4 large plum tomatoes, deseeded, skinned and roughly chopped
4 spring onions, finely chopped
1 large carrot, grated
1 fine-skinned courgette, grated
Spicy dressing for fish (see page 133)

1 Put the raisins into freshly boiled water for 1 minute. Drain.

2 Add the raisins to the couscous and cook according to packet instructions – this usually takes about 20 minutes – using stock instead of water.

3 Add the prawns and raw vegetables while the couscous is still hot. Pour on the dressing and stir to mix.

4 Serve while still warm, or cover with film and leave in the fridge. Bring back to room temperature before serving.

tuna fishcakes

Fishcakes are a perennial family favourite and taste just as good hot or cold. Two each is a substantial light meal, one makes an excellent starter. Oily fish like tuna is extremely heart- and skin-friendly because of the omega-3 fatty acids it contains. With the added nutritional value and cancer protection from the leafy green vegetables, you can turn a humble dish into a healthfest.

200g (7oz) potatoes, peeled
275g (10oz) green leafy vegetables – kale, spring greens, cabbage,
*   spinach, pak choi, etc., shredded*
320g (11oz) canned tuna (preferably in spring water), drained
6 spring onions, finely chopped
3 free-range organic eggs
6 tablespoons flour
Rapeseed oil for frying
1 iceberg lettuce, shredded
1 quantity hot tomato salsa (see page 123)

1 Boil and roughly mash the potatoes.

2 Steam the green vegetables until tender – the timing will depend on the type of vegetables you're using.

3 Flake the tuna into a large bowl. Add the onions, potatoes and vegetable leaves and mix thoroughly.

4 Beat the eggs in a bowl.

5 Tip the flour into another bowl.

6 With your hands, mould the fish and potato mixture into 8 flat cakes. Dip each one first into the egg, then the flour.

7 Pour sufficient oil into a frying pan to reach halfway up the fishcakes and fry them, in batches, over a medium heat, until golden – about 5 minutes each side.

8 Drain the fried fishcakes on a double layer of kitchen paper.

9 Divide the lettuce between 4 plates and drizzle with some of the salsa.

10 Put the fishcakes on top and serve with the rest of the salsa on the side.

ORAC value per serving ★↗
macaroni cheese

A favourite family standby, which provides lots of calcium and protein, with the bonus of betacarotene and minerals from the peppers and all of the heart– and circulatory–protection of garlic and onions. The addition of red peppers and parsley gives this far more eye appeal than ordinary macaroni cheese, and the paprika spices up what can sometimes be a rather bland dish.

225g (8oz) wholewheat macaroni
25g (1oz) unsalted butter
1 large onion, finely chopped
3 garlic cloves, finely chopped
2 large red peppers, deseeded and diced
1 teaspoon paprika
600ml (1 pint) milk
225g (8oz) mature Cheddar cheese
2 tablespoons freshly grated Parmesan cheese
Parsley leaves, finely chopped
Freshly ground black pepper

1 Cook the macaroni according to packet instructions. Drain and return to the rinsed pan.

2 Melt the butter in a frying pan. Add the onion and garlic and soften for 5 minutes. Tip into the macaroni.

3 Mix in the peppers and paprika.

4 Add the milk and cook, stirring continuously, for 10 minutes.

5 Tip in the Cheddar and Parmesan cheeses and stir until thoroughly mixed and the cheese has melted. Sprinkle with the parsley and season to taste with freshly ground black pepper.

ORAC value per serving ★↗
spinach snack-attack

I've known the faddiest of child eaters to eat these spinach snacks, and although the iron in this wonderful vegetable isn't well-absorbed, its antioxidant value and betacarotene content make it one of the most valuable of green-leafed vegetables. Add the lycopene and vitamin C from the tomatoes, sustaining carbohydrates, B vitamins and fibre from the bread and you have a delicious light lunch or late supper.

500g (1lb) baby spinach
25g (1oz) unsalted butter
2 tablespoons extra-virgin olive oil
2 garlic cloves, finely chopped
110g (4oz) pine nuts
Juice of 1 lemon
4 tomatoes, sliced
4 large slices thick wholemeal bread

1 Wash the spinach and put it into a pan with only the water clinging to it. Add the butter, cover tightly, put on a medium heat and, shaking the pan occasionally, leave until wilted – this should take no longer than 5 minutes.

2 Meanwhile, heat the oil in a frying pan and sauté the garlic and pine nuts gently until just turning golden. Add them to the cooked spinach with the lemon juice.

3 Place the tomato slices on the bread and top with the spinach mixture.

ORAC value per serving ★↵

welsh rarebit with sautéed apple and blueberries

Here's another family favourite with a bonus. The simple addition of apples, blueberries and onions not only results in a succulent, sweet-and-sour flavour, but adds vitamins, minerals and fibre to this protein- and calcium-rich dish.

110g (4oz) unsalted butter
4 large Cox's apples, peeled, cored and sliced
110g (4oz) blueberries
110g (4oz) Cheddar cheese, grated
1 large onion, finely grated
1 teaspoon dry mustard
200ml (7fl oz) stout
4 large slices wholemeal bread

1 Melt half the butter in a large frying pan.

2 Add the apples and cook on a medium heat until golden. Reduce the heat slightly, add the blueberries on one side of the pan and continue cooking for 5 minutes, turning the blueberries gently.

3 Put the cheese and onion into another pan with the mustard and stout. Stir until well combined and cook gently for 2 minutes.

4 Toast the bread on one side. Turn over, pile on the cheese mixture and grill for 5 minutes.

5 Meanwhile, place equal amounts of the apple and blueberry mixture on the side of 4 plates. Put the Welsh rarebit alongside and serve.

ORAC value per serving ★↵

stuffed celery and chicory

Despite the fact that cottage cheese is very low in fat and calories, the thought of eating one more portion brings a tear to the eye of anyone who has battled with weight-loss diets. Its boring texture and bland flavour don't make it food for the gourmet. But mix it with a hint of chives, the crunchiness of carrots, the sweetness of raisins and the peppery flavour of cancer-protective watercress and mustard and cress, finished with the iron-rich bitterness of chicory, and it's food to titillate the most jaded palate.

110g (4oz) seedless raisins
225g (8oz) cottage cheese
2 carrots, grated
12 chives, snipped
1 bunch or bag watercress, about 100g (3¹/₂oz), chopped
2 heads chicory, separated into leaves
4 thick sticks celery, cut into 5cm (2in) pieces
1 punnet mustard and cress

1 Soak the raisins in simmering water for 5 minutes. Drain and mix into the cottage cheese.

2 Add the carrot, chives and watercress, and mix again.

3 Arrange the celery and chicory leaves onto 4 plates.

4 Pile the cottage cheese mixture onto the chicory leaves and celery.

5 Sprinkle with the mustard and cress, and serve.

ORAC value per serving ★★

pasta with anchovy, garlic and lemon sauce

An instant non-cook sauce, with vitamin D and essential fatty acids from the anchovies, lycopene from the sun-dried and fresh tomatoes, bioflavonoids and vitamin C from the lemon, lots of energy from the pasta and the cleansing benefits of parsley and chives.

450g (12oz) spaghettini
8 slices sun-dried tomatoes
2 tablespoons capers
220g (8oz) canned or bottled anchovy fillets
2 garlic cloves, crushed
Grated rind and juice of 1 large lemon
6 tablespoons extra-virgin olive oil
4 large, fresh tomatoes, roughly chopped
3 large sprigs parsley, chopped
12 spears chives, snipped

1 Put the pasta on to cook according to packet instructions. Meanwhile, soak the sun-dried tomatoes in freshly boiled water for 5 minutes. Drain, chop finely and set aside.

3 Soak the capers in milk for 5 minutes, then drain.

4 Drain most of the oil off the anchovies. Put the fish into a mortar or mixing bowl, add the capers, garlic and grated lemon rind, and crush with a pestle or fork.

5 As the mixture starts to break down, pour in the lemon juice. Add the olive oil gradually, stirring, until the mixture forms a paste.

6 Add the paste to the drained pasta and mix well.

7 Stir in the drained sun-dried tomatoes and the fresh tomatoes, scatter the parsley and chives over the top, and serve.

ORAC value per serving ★★★★

tomato, mozzarella and avocado salad

A far cry from the ubiquitous tricolore salad of Italian restaurants in 1970s. Here the slabs of red tomato, white mozzarella and green avocado are complemented by the hugely nutritious dried fruits, massive amounts of vitamin C from the kiwi and an extremely high ORAC score. A salad to turn back your biological clock.

175g (6oz) mixed dried fruits – dates, stoneless prunes, apricots,
*   raisins, etc.– cut into raisin-sized pieces*
2 quantities standard French dressing (see page 132)
350g (12oz) fresh, young mozzarella cheese, drained and cubed
4 large tomatoes, roughly chopped
2 avocados, peeled, stoned and cubed

1 Soak all the fruits in freshly boiled water for 5 minutes. Drain thoroughly and stir into the dressing.

2 Tip the tomato, mozzarella and avocado into a large bowl

3 Pour the fruit dressing over the top and pour well.

main
courses

All recipes in this chapter serve 4 .

ORAC value per serving ★↗

fusilli with tomato sauce

This non-meat dish is a one-pot meal with a good ORAC score and an exceptionally high anti-cancer value thanks to the cabbage, kale and leeks, and the lycopene in the tomato sauce.

1 litre (1³/4 pints) basic stock (see page 30) or stock made with
  salt-free stock cubes
400g (14oz) tricolore fusilli
¹/4 large savoy cabbage, roughly chopped
2 large leeks, roughly chopped
4 large leaves kale, roughly chopped
400ml (14fl oz) fresh tomato sauce (see page 122)
1 large avocado

1 Bring the stock to the boil in a large saucepan.

2 Add the fusilli and chopped green vegetables and simmer until the pasta is just tender.

3 Meanwhile, heat the tomato sauce.

4 Peel and stone the avocado and mash the flesh.

5 Remove the tomato sauce from the heat and mix in the avocado until blended.

6 Drain the pasta and vegetables and put into a large bowl. Serve with the tomato and avocado mixture on top.

ORAC value per serving ★★↗

dutch indonesian lamb

When I first tasted Dutch East Indian food as a small boy visiting my uncle in Holland, the strange mixture of meat with peanut sauce was surprising. Now, this melange of flavours is commonplace, but no less delicious for that. This combination of warm lamb and salad is easy to cook and a fun dish to serve to friends, as you have to pick up the chops with your fingers – always an ice-breaker.

1 small red pepper, deseeded and roughly sliced
6 ready-to-eat dates, quartered
2 tablespoons crunchy peanut butter
1 tablespoon tahini
1 teaspoon soy sauce
2 garlic cloves
Up to 5 tablespoons extra-virgin olive oil
2 racks of lamb, 6–8 chops each
About 150g (5oz) mixed green salad leaves
1 quantity standard French dressing (see page 132)

1 Put the pepper, dates, peanut butter, tahini, soy sauce and garlic into a blender and whizz, adding olive oil as necessary to keep the mixture smooth.

2 Pull most of the thick fat layer off the meaty part of the lamb. Rub the mixture over the meat and leave in the fridge for about 1 hour to let the flavours combine.

3 Set the oven to its maximum temperature. When it reaches that heat, take the rack of lamb out of the fridge and put in the oven with the peanut mixture still on top. Turn down the heat to 200°C/400°F/gas mark 6 and roast for 35 minutes.

4 Remove from the oven, cover loosely with foil and leave to rest for 10 minutes.

5 Meanwhile, wash the salad leaves and toss in the salad dressing.

6 Cut the rack of lamb into chops. Put the salad on a serving plate and arrange the lamb chops on top.

ORAC value per serving ★★✔

mango chicken

More taste of the Pacific Rim as the exotic flavours of mango are combined with simple roast chicken. As well as the high-ORAC value, the walnuts provide additional heart protection from their monounsaturated fats. The sweetness is offset by the bite of rocket.

1 small, cold roast chicken
2 ripe mangoes, cubed
Juice of 2 limes
4 large spring onions, finely sliced
110g (4oz) raisins
100ml (3¹/₂fl oz) extra-virgin olive oil
6 teaspoons organic mayonnaise
50g (2oz) walnuts, chopped
200g (7oz) rocket, torn

1 Roughly chop the chicken flesh, discarding the skin and bones.

2 Mix the chicken, mangoes, lime juice, spring onions and raisins with the oil and mayonnaise.

3 Add the walnuts and rocket.

4 Stir all the ingredients together and serve.

ORAC value per serving ★

pasta arabiata

Sometimes called diabolo – devil's sauce – because it can be devilishly hot, it's the chilli that stimulates the circulation and the garlic, sweetcorn and fresh herbs that generate the useful ORAC score of this pasta.

3 garlic cloves, chopped
Leaves of 3 sprigs fresh parsley
4 sprigs fresh oregano or marjoram, left whole
1 teaspoon chilli powder
¹/₂ teaspoon cayenne pepper
4 tablespoons extra-virgin olive oil
2 teaspoons red wine vinegar
2 tablespoons tomato purée
3 large flat mushrooms
2 courgettes, cut into 2.5cm (1in) slices
200g (7oz) frozen sweetcorn
450g (1lb) dried penne
3 tablespoons freshly grated Parmesan cheese

1 Put the garlic, parsley, oregano or marjoram, chilli powder, cayenne pepper, olive oil and vinegar into a blender and whizz for 1 minute until smooth.

2 Add the tomato purée and 2 teaspoons of water and whizz for 3 seconds.

3 Add mushrooms, courgettes and sweetcorn to the blender and whizz for 1 minute, adding water if the sauce looks too thick.

4 Cook the penne according to instructions on the packet, or until al dente. Drain.

5 Over a low heat, warm the purée until it just begins to bubble. Stir it into the hot pasta and serve sprinkled with the Parmesan.

200g (7oz) canned chickpeas, drained
4 large sprigs flat-leaf parsley, finely chopped
Juice of 1 large lemon
4 small salmon trout, trimmed and gutted
150ml (5fl oz) dry white wine
50g (2oz) unsalted butter

1 Preheat the oven to 220°C/425°F/gas mark 7.

2 Heat the oil in a frying pan, add the onions and garlic, and sweat gently for 5 minutes.

3 Stir in the paprika and cayenne pepper and cook for a further 2 minutes.

4 Add the tomatoes and chickpeas and simmer until tender – about 10 minutes.

5 Mash the mixture roughly, pouring off any excess tomato juice until you have the consistency of a stuffing.

6 Add the parsley and lemon juice and mix into the stuffing.

7 Pile the stuffing into the trout cavities.

8 Cut 4 pieces of kitchen foil big enough to totally envelop each fish. Put each trout on a piece of foil. Divide the wine among them, dot with the butter, season generously with coarsely-ground black pepper and seal the parcels.

9 Bake for 20 minutes. Open the foil carefully to let the steam escape before serving.

ORAC value per serving ★↵

baked stuffed trout

Trout is such good nutritional value for money and so easily available, but I think people get bored with having it just plain, steamed, grilled or pan-fried with almonds. Do try this interesting and extremely healthy recipe with distinct overtones of the Middle East.

4 tablespoons extra-virgin olive oil
1 small onion, finely chopped
1 garlic clove, finely chopped
1 teaspoon paprika
1 teaspoon cayenne pepper
220g (8oz) canned chopped tomatoes

ORAC value per serving ★★

californian risotto

You can't make risotto in a hurry, but the whole ethos of 'slow food' is the use of traditional methods to conserve flavour, texture and nutrients. Cooking risotto is as therapeutic as any form of meditation and more relaxing than a bucket full of Prozac. The only side effect is the substantial health benefit of the high ORAC score.

1 tablespoon extra-virgin olive oil
2 garlic cloves, chopped
5 spring onions, chopped
2 small red chillies, deseeded and finely diced
1 small red pepper, deseeded and finely diced
1 small yellow pepper, deseeded and finely diced
200g (7oz) arborio rice
1 tablespoon ground coriander
2 tablespoons ground cumin
About 850ml (1 1/2 pints) basic stock (see page 30)
225g (8oz) ready-to-eat prunes, snipped into 5mm (1/4in) pieces
Leaves of 3 large sprigs parsley, chopped
Leaves of 3 large sprigs coriander, chopped

1 Heat the oil gently in a deep frying pan or saucepan, add the garlic, onions, chillies and peppers and simmer until soft – about 10 minutes.

2 Mix in the rice and stir until coated with the oil.

3 Add the coriander and cumin, and cook for 3 minutes, stirring continuously.

4 Add a ladleful of stock, stirring until the liquid is absorbed.

5 Add the prunes to the rice mixture with the second ladleful of stock.

6 Continue adding stock, a ladleful at a time, for about 20 minutes, until the rice is tender but still has some bite.

7 Serve with the chopped parsley and coriander leaves scattered on top.

ORAC value per serving ★★

sally's vegetarian sunshine bake

Here is the essence of the Mediterranean diet. It's not just the vitamins A, C and E that you get from the oil and fresh vegetables, but the anti-oxidant properties in onions, garlic, aubergines and tomatoes that make this such a protective dish. There's a bonus from calcium in the cheese and antibacterial essential oils in the oregano. Health benefits aside, this dish smells wonderful when it's cooking and it looks like a plate of sunshine.

6 tablespoons olive oil

3 sweet Spanish onions, diced

2 garlic cloves, finely chopped

3 large sprigs fresh oregano, roughly chopped. Fresh oregano is
   widely available. Dried won't be as good for aroma or
   flavour, but if you have to use it, add 1 tablespoon

2 smallish aubergines, cut into 5mm (1/4in) slices

5 courgettes, peeled if necessary and cut into 5mm (1/4in) slices

6 tomatoes, cut into 5mm (1/4in) slices

450g (1lb) fresh, young mozzarella cheese, cut into
   5mm (1/4in) slices

5 tablespoons freshly grated Parmesan

6 sprigs dill

Freshly ground black pepper

1   Preheat the oven to 200°C/400°F/ gas mark 6.

2   Heat the oil in a frying pan, add the onions and cook gently for 5 minutes to soften.

3   Add the garlic and continue cooking for 3 minutes.

4   Stir the oregano into the onion mixture and remove from the heat.

5   Put the aubergine slices on a baking tray in a single layer, sprinkle with salt and bake for 8 minutes until softened.

6   Put the onion and herb mixture into an ovenproof dish. Arrange the aubergine, courgette, tomato and mozzarella alternately in the dish, standing them on their sides. When they're all arranged, push down gently with the palms of your hands and season with black pepper.

7   Place the dish in the oven and bake for about 1 hour.

8   Sprinkle the Parmesan on top and bake for another 10 minutes.

9   Serve with the whole sprigs of dill scattered on top.

ORAC value per serving ★★★✦

vegetarian nutty bake

This is nut roast with attitude. The combined nutritional value of the root vegetables, prunes, oats and other ingredients makes this a health-plus recipe, which will be enjoyed as much by committed carnivores as it will be by the vehement veggies. This is super-ORAC food.

75g (3oz) unsalted butter
1 onion, finely chopped
2 garlic cloves, finely chopped
350g (12oz) mixed root vegetables – carrots, turnips, potatoes, etc.
  – peeled and finely diced
1 leek, cut into 5mm (1/4in) slices
2 courgettes, cubed
200g (7oz) chestnut mushrooms, sliced
50g (2oz) wholemeal flour
300ml (1/2 pint) basic vegetable stock (see page 30)
4 tablespoons tomato purée
100g (4oz) ready-to-eat prunes, quartered
2 large sprigs curly parsley, finely chopped
75g (3oz) porridge oats
75g (3oz) crushed mixed nuts
Freshly ground black pepper

1 Preheat the oven to 180°C/350°F/gas mark 4.

2 Melt 50g (2oz) of the butter in a large frying pan.

3 Gently sweat the onion and garlic in the butter until soft – about 5 minutes.

4 Add the root vegetables to the pan and continue cooking gently for another 10 minutes.

5 Add the leek, courgettes and mushrooms to the pan and cook for 1 minute.

6 Stir in the flour and cook for 1 minute, stirring continuously.

7 Pour in the stock, tomato purée and prunes and stir until thickened.

8 Add the parsley to the mixture, season well with freshly ground black pepper and pour the mixture into an ovenproof dish.

9 Rub the remaining butter into the oats and nuts, scatter on top of the dish and bake for 30 minutes.

ORAC value per serving ★★★

duck breasts in onion and fruit sauce

This unusual way of cooking duck is extremely simple. It's a perfect dish if you're entertaining as you can prepare it in advance and reheat it when you're ready. It provides excellent protein and a massively protective ORAC score thanks to the prunes and cranberries. You'll find ready-prepared duck breasts in most supermarkets.

110g (4oz) dried cranberries
4 duck breasts
4 tablespoons olive oil
2 large Spanish onions, finely diced
2 tablespoons wholemeal flour
200ml (7fl oz) orange juice
150ml (5fl oz) dry white wine
2 large sprigs fresh thyme, finely chopped
75g (3oz) ready-to-eat prunes, cut into cranberry-size pieces

1 Pour enough boiling water over the cranberries just to cover them. Leave in a bowl.

2 Trim any fat off the duck breasts and flatten slightly with the back of a wooden spoon.

3 Heat half the oil in a large frying pan and brown the duck breasts on both sides. Drain off the fat, transfer to a warm plate and reserve.

4 Clean the pan and heat the remaining oil in it. Add the onions and sauté gently for 5 minutes.

5 Add the flour and cook gently, stirring continuously, for another 2 minutes.

6 Drain the cranberries, reserving the liquid.

7 Over a gentle heat, gradually pour the orange juice, wine and cranberry liquid into the onion and flour mixture.

8 Add the duck breasts, thyme, prunes and cranberries to the pan. Cover and simmer for about 30 minutes, until the duck is tender.

ORAC value per serving ★★✦

chicken and prunes

The carrot, courgette and fresh herbs are all good sources of ORAC, but the addition of dried fruit and garlic makes this recipe the highly protective dish that it is – and also provides its North African flavours.

4 skinless chicken breasts

4 tablespoons lemon juice

4 tablespoons extra-virgin olive oil

2 sprigs tarragon, left whole

4 bay leaves

2 large carrots, peeled and sliced

3 courgettes, sliced lengthways

200ml (7fl oz) basic stock (see page 30) or chicken stock from the chicken soup recipe (see page 40)

6 ready-to-eat stoneless prunes

6 no-need-to-soak dried apricots

2 garlic cloves, finely chopped

35g (1½oz) fresh breadcrumbs

2 tablespoons chopped fresh mixed herbs: tarragon, flat-leaf parsley, chervil and oregano

1 Flatten the chicken breasts with the back of a wooden spoon and put them into a deep ovenproof dish large enough to hold them in one layer. Cover with the lemon juice and 3 tablespoons of the oil.

2 Add the tarragon and bay leaves. Place in the fridge for at least 1 hour, turning once. Remove the bay leaves.

3 Preheat the oven to 200°C/400°F/gas mark 6.

4 Arrange the carrots and courgettes on the chicken, basting them with the marinade.

5 Add the stock, prunes and apricots, cover with foil and cook in the oven until tender – about 40 minutes.

6 Meanwhile heat the remaining oil in a frying pan and gently sauté the garlic.

7 Add the breadcrumbs and stir until golden, then stir in the mixed herbs.

8 Sprinkle the herb mixture over the chicken dish and serve.

ORAC value per serving ★★★✦

trout with prune relish

Here's another interesting way to cook trout, which is also going to supply the majority of your day's ORAC needs for optimum protection. Making the prune relish is simple, and the finished dish has a wonderful richness. This prune relish goes equally well with other robust fish, game, rabbit, duck, goose or ham.

Juice of 2 lemons
2 sprigs coriander, finely chopped
3 tablespoons olive oil
3 bay leaves
4 trout fillets
35g (1¹/₂oz) unsalted butter
75g (3oz) chopped mixed nuts
4 large spring onions, chopped
2 garlic cloves, chopped
100ml (3¹/₂fl oz) white wine vinegar, cider vinegar or rice vinegar
3 plum tomatoes, chopped
15 stoned ready-to-eat prunes, chopped

1 Mix half the lemon juice and half the coriander with the oil. Add the bay leaves, pour over the trout and leave in the fridge for 1 hour.

2 Remove the fish from the marinade and reserve the liquid.

3 Put the fish on a grill pan, brush with the marinade and grill for about 5 minutes each side, basting every minute or so.

4 Meanwhile, melt the butter in a frying pan. Add the nuts and sauté for 2 minutes. **5** Add the onions and garlic to the pan with the vinegar and the rest of the lemon juice and cook gently for a further 2 minutes.

6 Add the tomatoes and prunes with the rest of the coriander, and cook for another 2 minutes.

7 Serve the trout with the relish on top.

ORAC value per serving ★★

persian beef stew

There has been a remarkable renaissance of traditional Persian cooking in the last few years, and family-run Persian, rather than Iranian, restaurants have sprung up in many major cities. The cooking is healthy and the savoury dishes are deliciously flavoured with spices like cinnamon and nutmeg, more usually associated with sweet meals.

110g (4oz) yellow split peas (rinse, put into water for 10 minutes & drain)
1 tablespoon extra-virgin olive oil
1 large onion, finely chopped
350g (12oz) lean stewing beef, trimmed of fat and cubed
1 teaspoon ground cinnamon
¹/₄ teaspoon grated nutmeg
600ml (1 pint) basic stock (see page 30)
1 large cooking apple, peeled, cored and thickly sliced
1 sweet potato, peeled and cubed
Juice of 1 lemon
75g (3oz) raisins
110g (4oz) frozen peas
2 tablespoons runny honey
Salt and pepper

1 Put the split peas in a bowl, cover with water, and leave for 1 hour.

2 Heat the oil in a large, deep frying pan, add the onion and soften gently for 3 minutes.

3 Add the meat and continue cooking, stirring continuously, until the meat is sealed and the onion becomes slightly golden.

4 Stir in the cinnamon and nutmeg, add the stock and simmer, covered, for 30 minutes.

5 Drain and rinse the split peas. Put into a saucepan of boiling water and boil for 5 minutes. Drain.

6 Add the split peas to the pan with the apple and potato. Bring back to the boil, cover and simmer for 15 minutes.

7 Add the lemon juice, honey, raisins and green peas, pushing the raisins and the peas into the pan without breaking up the apple. Continue to simmer for 15–20 minutes.

8 Season with salt and pepper if necessary, and serve.

ORAC value per serving ★★

three bean, aubergine and tofu casserole

It really isn't necessary to go to all the trouble of salting and pressing aubergines before you cook them – something I think puts people off using this wonderful, high-ORAC vegetable. Tofu is another food that makes people turn up their noses, but as well as having a useful ORAC rating, it's about the best source of natural plant hormones, which have special protective benefits of their own. The delicious flavours of sesame, coconut and coriander make this dish well worth a try, so put aside your prejudices and be prepared for a pleasant surprise.

2 tablespoons extra-virgin olive oil
25g (1oz) unsalted butter
1 red onion, chopped
2 garlic cloves, chopped
1/2 teaspoon chilli powder
1/2 large aubergine, peeled and diced
110g (4oz) French beans, cut into 2.5cm (1in) pieces
110g (4oz) broad beans
220g (8oz) canned kidney beans, rinsed and drained
225g (8oz) tofu, cubed
400ml (14fl oz) coconut milk
400ml (14fl oz) basic stock (see page 30)

1 Preheat the oven to to 200°C/400°F/gas mark 6.

2 Heat the oil and butter in a frying pan and soften the onion and garlic in it for about 5 minutes.

3 Add the chilli powder and continue cooking for 1 minute.

4 Add the aubergine to the pan and cook for 2 minutes.

5 Transfer the contents of the pan to a casserole dish, and add the French beans, broad beans, kidney beans and tofu.

6 Pour on the coconut milk and stock, adding more stock if necessary to cover the ingredients.

7 Bake for 40 minutes, checking occasionally to ensure the casserole isn't drying out.

ORAC value per serving ★↗

calves' liver with almonds

Although not exceptionally high in ORAC value, this is one of my favourite ways of cooking liver. We're very lucky to have Joe Collier and his award-winning butcher's shop, Eastwoods, just a few miles away in Berkhamsted. Although organic calves' liver is expensive, it's worth every penny for its lack of unwanted toxic chemicals and its fabulous flavour. It also supplies masses of vitamins A and B12, and iron.

Leaves of 1 large sprig rosemary, finely chopped
2 garlic cloves, very finely chopped
110g (4oz) fresh wholemeal breadcrumbs
110g (4oz) ground almonds
2 pinches ground saffron
4 tablespoons extra-virgin olive oil
50g (2oz) unsalted butter

4 slices calves' liver, about 175g (6oz) each
150ml (5fl oz) red wine
110g (4oz) raisins
Freshly ground black pepper
Steamed carrots and broccoli, to serve

1 Mix the rosemary, garlic, breadcrumbs, almonds and saffron into half the oil. Season with black pepper.

2 Heat the butter and remaining oil in a large frying pan. Add the liver and cook for 3–4 minutes, depending on thickness and how pink you like it, turning once. Remove and keep warm.

3 Put all the other ingredients into the pan and boil briskly for 2 minutes, stirring to loosen any liver stuck to the bottom.

4 Serve the liver with the sauce spooned over the top and accompanied by steamed carrots and broccoli.

ORAC value per serving ★★★

curried bean and root vegetable stew

This is a perfect autumn or winter dish. It takes, at most, 30 minutes to prepare and is an ideal recipe for a slow cooker. Get it ready the night before, put into the slow cooker before you leave for work and when you open the door in the evening, you'll be greeted by mouth-watering smells, bursting with ORAC to protect against winter chills and ills.

3 tablespoons rapeseed oil – ideally organic, but GM-free at least
1 large leek, sliced
1 large onion, chopped
3 garlic cloves, finely chopped
3 teaspoons good curry powder or paste
1 swede, cubed
1 large parsnip, cubed
2 carrots, cubed
1 sweet potato, peeled and cubed
About 700ml (1¼ pints)) basic stock (see page 30)
400g (14oz) canned organic crushed tomatoes
3 tablespoons tomato purée
400g (14oz) canned broad beans, rinsed and drained

1 In a large saucepan, heat the oil and sweat the leek, onion and garlic, stirring continuously, for 3 minutes.

2 Tip in the curry powder or paste, stir until it coats the vegetables and cook for another 2 minutes. Add the root vegetables to the pan and stir to coat thoroughly. Add the stock, crushed tomatoes and tomato purée and bring to the boil. Cover and simmer for 45 minutes.

4 Add the broad beans and continue to simmer until beans and vegetable are all tender – about 10–15 minutes.

ORAC value per serving ★★★★★★★

braised duck with prunes

Here's a recipe that's a poke in the nose for all those food police who try to persuade everyone that healthy eating should be the culinary equivalent of sackcloth and ashes. The combined flavours of duck, shallots, Armagnac and prunes are worthy of any Michelin-star restaurant, but the recipe is simplicity itself. It's full of protein, the heart-protective benefits of garlic, shallots and red wine, lots of fibre from the dried fruit and huge amounts of betacarotene. Add a simple salad for vitamin C and you'll have everything your body needs – with an extraordinarily high ORAC score.

2 tablespoons extra-virgin olive oil
4 duck breasts
110g (4oz) bacon cubes
200g (7oz) shallots, quartered
3 tablespoons Armagnac
2 tablespoons flour
600ml (1 pint) red wine
10 prunes, stoned
10 dried apricots
3 garlic cloves, finely chopped
1 bouquet garni

1 Preheat the oven to 220°C/425°F/gas mark 7.

2 Heat the oil in a frying pan and brown the duck breasts on both sides. Remove and keep warm.

3 Brown the bacon and shallots in the pan.

4 Return the duck to the pan, pour on the Armagnac and set alight. When the flames die down completely, stir in the flour and mix thoroughly.

5 Transfer the contents of the pan to a casserole dish.

6 Add half the wine to the frying pan, with the prunes, apricots, garlic and bouquet garni. Bring to the boil, then add to the casserole dish. Pour in the rest of the wine and bake for 20 minutes.

ORAC value per serving ★★✦

new orleans herb gumbo

This is a very traditional Creole vegetarian gumbo, redolent of the hot, steamy swamplands and the flavours of allspice and cloves. This style of New Orleans cooking was born out of poverty and, like all peasant food, it's nourishing, filling and sustaining. It's also exceptionally protective.

75g (3oz) fine wholemeal flour
6 garlic cloves
2 tablespoons extra-virgin olive oil
1 large onion, chopped
1 red pepper, deseeded and cubed
2 large sticks celery, sliced
2 pinches allspice
225g (8oz) long-grain rice
1.3kg (3lb) mixed green leafy vegetables – spinach, spring greens,
*   cabbage, kale, chard, Brussels sprouts, etc.*
3 bay leaves
1 teaspoon dried basil
1 teaspoon dried thyme
2 pinches ground cloves
Leaves of 1 large sprig curly parsley, chopped
2 pinches cayenne pepper
1 teaspoon liquid seasoning, such as Kallo or Maggi
600ml (1 pint) hot tomato salsa (see page 123)
Salt and pepper

1 Brown the flour by heating gently in a dry frying pan, stirring constantly. Remove and reserve.

2 Finely chop 3 of the garlic cloves.

3 Heat the oil in a saucepan, add the chopped garlic, onion, pepper and celery, and sweat until soft – about 5 minutes.

4 Add the browned flour and allspice, stir well and set aside.

5 In a separate saucepan, put the rice on to cook, following packet instructions.

6 Mash the remaining garlic cloves.

7 In another pan, cook all the greens in just enough water to cover, with the mashed garlic, bay leaves, basil, thyme and ground cloves for 5 minutes.

8 Drain, reserving the cooking liquid, and chop. Remove the bay leaves and any large pieces of garlic.

9 Gradually add about 400ml (15fl oz) of the vegetable water to the flour mixture, adding extra water if necessary to make up the quantity. Stir constantly over a low heat until completely smooth.

10 Pour the mixture over the greens and stir thoroughly. Season, mix in the parsley, cayenne pepper and liquid seasoning thoroughly.

11 Drain the rice and pour the vegetable mixture on top. Serve with the hot tomato salsa on the side.

ORAC value per serving ★★✦

ham and kidney bean gumbo

Another great gumbo from the Louisiana bayous, which typifies the culinary melting pot of the Choctaw Indians, the Cajuns, the French and the awful heritage of the African slave trade. Tradition tells us that this recipe was referred to as 'washday gumbo', served on Monday, when the women were too busy with the washing to spend hours cooking. It was prepared when they had time on Sunday and, like so many stews, tasted even better the following day. This recipe is extremely rich in a wide variety of nutrients.

225g (8oz) brown rice
2 tablespoons sunflower oil
1 red onion, chopped
2 garlic cloves, chopped
1 stick celery, sliced
1 small green pepper, deseeded and cubed
1 small red pepper, deseeded and cubed
225g (8oz) piece lean ham, finely cubed
600g (1¹/4lb) canned kidney beans, rinsed and drained
¹/2 teaspoon dried thyme
¹/2 teaspoon dried oregano
1¹/2 litres (2¹/2 pints) basic stock (see page 30)
1 tablespoon liquid seasoning, such as Kallo or Maggi
1 teaspoon Tabasco sauce

1 Put the rice on to cook according to packet instructions. If it's done before the gumbo is ready, drain, cover and keep warm.

2 Heat the oil in a large saucepan and sauté the onion and garlic gently until softened.

3 Add the celery and peppers and continue sautéing gently for 4 minutes.

4 Add the ham and continue to sauté for another 4 minutes.

5 Mix in the beans, herbs, stock, liquid seasoning and Tabasco, and simmer until the beans are tender – 5–10 minutes.

6 Drain the rice and serve the gumbo on top.

ORAC value per serving ✦

veggie honey-roast tofu

Not a very high ORAC recipe, but extremely rich in the soy-isoflavones – plant hormones that are especially protective for women against breast cancer, osteoporosis and the discomforts of the menopause. It also has a good level of fibre from the root vegetables and a healthy balance of omega-3 and omega–6 fatty acids from the rapeseed oil. Boost the ORAC rating with any of the sauces or compôtes in 'Sauces, Marinades and Compôtes'.

4 tablespoons rapeseed oil – ideally organic, but absolutely
  GM-free
3 tablespoons honey
3 tablespoons light soy sauce
1 parsnip, cut into bite-sized cubes
1 sweet potato, peeled and cut into bite-sized cubes
1 large red apple, peeled, cored and cut into bite-sized cube
225g (8oz) tofu, cubed
Freshly ground black pepper

t1 Preheat the oven to190°C/375°F/gas mark 5.

2 Brush a baking tray with some of the oil.

3 Put the rest of the oil in a small saucepan and melt the honey in it over a low heat. Add the soy sauce.

4 Put the vegetables and apple into a bowl, pour in half the soy sauce mixture and stir to coat thoroughly.

5 Transfer to the baking tray, cover with foil and put in the oven to roast, stirring occasionally

6 Meanwhile, put the tofu in the rest of the sauce, making up an extra quantity if needed and adding 3 good twists of fresh, coarsely ground black pepper. Leave to marinate.

7 After 40 minutes, add the tofu to the baking tray and return to the oven, uncovered, for another 20 minutes.

ORAC value per serving ★★✦

gvetch: romanian one-pot vegetable stew

Another truly peasant recipe, named after the gvetch pot in which it is cooked. Made without meat – an expensive luxury for agricultural workers – this wonderful mixture of fresh and dried beans, green and root vegetables provides protein for growth, carbohydrates for energy and plenty of vitamins and minerals. It's also a high ORAC dish.

1 small sweet onion, chopped
2 garlic cloves, chopped
1 small white potato, peeled and sliced
1 small sweet potato, peeled and sliced
1/4 small green cabbage, such as savoy, coarsely chopped
50g (2oz) button mushrooms, halved
1 bay leaf
1 small carrot, cut into 2.5cm (1in) pieces
1/2 stick of celery, cut into 2.5cm (1in) pieces
1 small green pepper, deseeded and diced
1 head broccoli, cut into florets
1/2 aubergine, sliced
225g (8oz) canned lima beans, rinsed and drained
Leaves of 2 large sprigs flat-leaf parsley, chopped
50g (2oz) fresh French beans, sliced into thirds
1 tomato, thinly sliced
300ml (10fl oz) tomato juice
Salt and pepper

1 Layer in a narrow, deep saucepan all the ingredients from onion to French beans in the order they appear in the list above.

2 Arrange the tomato slices on top.

3 Pour on the tomato juice.

4 Cover the pan and bring slowly to a simmer. Cook, tightly covered, for about 30 minutes, adding water if the mixture seems to be drying out.

5 Leave to rest for 15 minutes and add salt and pepper as necessary.

ORAC value per serving ★★

fish risotto

This is one of our family favourites for a light, nourishing, late supper on Fridays after a long and busy week. Sally has this recipe down to a T and the delicious crunchy texture of the mange tout, with the softness of the rice and fish, blends perfectly with the Asian flavour of curry. Excellent nutrition and a good ORAC recipe, too.

2 tablespoons rapeseed oil – preferably organic, but certainly GM-free
1 onion, chopped
1 garlic clove, finely chopped
2 teaspoons curry powder
1 small red pepper, deseeded and diced
225g (8oz) arborio rice
450ml (16fl oz) basic stock (see page 30)
450ml (16fl oz) coconut milk
350g (12oz) cod fillet or other firm fish such as hake, halibut, monkfish, haddock, fresh tuna or swordfish – or 225g (8oz) fish and 110g (4oz) cooked peeled prawns
75g (3oz) very young mange tout, cut into 1.5cm (1/2in) lengths
220g (8oz) canned sweetcorn, rinsed and drained
Leaves of 6 sprigs flat-leaf parsley, coarsely chopped

1 Heat the oil in a deep frying pan or saucepan and gently sauté the onion and garlic until soft – about 5 minutes.

2 Stir in the curry powder, mix thoroughly and cook for 2 minutes.

3 Add the red pepper, rice, stock and coconut milk, and simmer for 20 minutes, until the rice is tender and nearly all the liquid has been absorbed.

4 Break the fish into bite-sized chunks, stir into the rice mixture, mix well and put back on a gentle heat for 5 minutes, adding more stock if the risotto looks as if it's drying out. Check that the firm fish is cooked – fish with denser flesh, monkfish and tuna particularly, may take a few minutes longer.

5 Add the mange tout, sweetcorn and prawns, if using, and heat through for 2 minutes. Serve the risotto with the parsley on top.

`ORAC value per serving` ★★✸

steamed fish in foil

A brilliantly easy way to cook fish and the healthiest way to cook the vegetables, this produces a finished dish that is extremely high in essential nutrients and has a simple, clean flavour. The impressive ORAC score is a bonus.

4 steaks of salmon, halibut or hake
2 small carrots, thinly sliced lengthways with a vegetable peeler
1 orange pepper, deseeded and cut into very fine strips
4 spring onions, sliced lengthways into strands
Juice of 1 lemon
150ml (5fl oz) dry white wine
50g (2oz) unsalted butter
4 sprigs dill
700g (1¹/₂lb) mixed green leafy vegetables – spinach, chard, cabbage, kale, etc. – coarsely chopped
2 leeks, very finely sliced
Freshly ground black pepper

1 Preheat the oven to 200°C/400°F/gas mark 6.

2 Cut 4 pieces of kitchen foil large enough to envelop each piece of fish comfortably. Put each fish steak into the middle of a piece of foil. Add the carrots, pepper and spring onions.

3 Pull up the sides of the parcels and pour in the wine and lemon juice. Dot each parcel with butter, lay the dill on top, add a twist of freshly ground black pepper and seal the parcels.

4 Bake in the oven for 20 minutes.

5 Meanwhile, put the green leafy vegetables into a steamer and cook until they're just tender but with bite – about 10 minutes.

6 When the fish is done, pile the green vegetables on individual serving plates. Carefully open one end of each parcel and pour the juices over the green vegetables. To serve, use a fish slice or spatula to lift the fish, with the vegetables on top, on to the green vegetables.

ORAC value per serving ★★

beef and couscous pilaff

Distinct flavours of North Africa enhance this substantial dish. The unique combination of pistachios, beef and spices is what produces the taste, but it's the addition of the peas and dried fruits that bump up the ORAC score. Including generous amounts of fresh mint improves digestion and offsets any fattiness in the beef.

Scant 1/2 teaspoon ground cumin
Scant 1/2 teaspoon ground cinnamon
1 teaspoon ground coriander
225g (8oz) lean braising steak, cut into small cubes
2 tablespoons rapeseed oil – preferably organic, but certainly GM-free
225g (8oz) couscous
75g (3oz) no-need-to-soak apricots, each cut into 6 pieces
75g (3oz) sultanas
700ml (1 1/2 pints) basic stock (see page 30)
75g (3oz) shelled pistachio nuts
110g (4oz) frozen peas
Leaves of 4 large sprigs mint, chopped

1 Mix the ground cumin and cinnamon and half the coriander.

2 Coat the meat with the spice mixture and set aside.

3 Heat half the oil in a large frying pan, pour in the couscous and cook, stirring continuously, for 2 minutes. Take off the heat and stir in the remaining coriander.

4 Add the apricots to the couscous with the sultanas.

5 Boil the stock and add half to the couscous, stir, cover and leave to stand for 10 minutes.

6 Meanwhile, dry fry the nuts gently for 5 minutes.

7 Fluff up the couscous with a fork and add the rest of the stock.

8 Cook the peas in boiling water for 2 minutes, sprinkle them on top of the couscous, cover and leave again.

9 Heat the remaining oil in another pan, seal the steak, turn down the heat slightly and continue cooking for 8 minutes, or until as well done as you like it, stirring continuously.

10 Add the meat and nuts to the couscous and stir thoroughly.

11 Sprinkle the mint over and serve.

ORAC value per serving ★★★✦

stir-fried vegetables with prawns

Like the French paradox and the Mediterranean diet, the way people eat in the Far East holds the secret of their good health. In this part of the world, women have less breast cancer, hardly any osteoporosis and there's not even a word for menopausal hot flushes. Heart disease, high blood pressure and bowel cancer are also comparatively rare. It's not just that they eat less meat, but much less fat, and pot noodles and burgers are, thankfully, still not part of their culinary culture. It's what they do eat that counts – and this great dish is a typical example.

1 tablespoon light soy sauce

1 tablespoon sherry vinegar

1/2 teaspoon tabasco sauce

1 tablespoon sesame oil

1 teaspoon runny honey

2 tablespoons rapeseed oil – preferably organic, but certainly
  GM-free

2 carrots, finely sliced

110g (4oz) oyster mushrooms, sliced

1 head broccoli, cut into uniform-sized florets

2 heads pak choi, cut into 8 lengthways

1.5cm (1/2in) fresh ginger root, peeled and grated

5 fat spring onions, quartered lengthways

150g (6oz) mange tout, cut into 2cm (3/4in) pieces

8 raw king tiger prawns in their shells

450g (1lb) fresh bean sprouts

4 tablespoons sesame seeds

1 Whisk together the soy sauce, sherry vinegar, tabasco sauce, sesame oil and runny honey and set aside.

2 Heat the rapeseed oil in a wok or large, deep-sided frying pan. Add the carrots, mushrooms, broccoli, pak choi and ginger and stir-fry, stirring continuously, for 3 minutes.

3 Add the spring onions and mange tout and continue cooking for 1 minute.

4 Tip in the prawns and cook for 4 minutes, until they start to change colour.

5 Tip in the beansprouts and cook for 1 minute.

6 Add the soy sauce mixture and 3 tablespoons water and cook gently until the vegetables are tender – about 4 minutes.

7 Meanwhile, dry fry the sesame seeds in a separate pan.

8 Serve the stir-fry with the sesame seeds scattered on top.

7

sweet
things

All recipes in this chapter serve 4 .

ORAC value per serving ★★★★★

fruity rice pudding

Rice pudding may sound like nursery food, but this one has a sophisticated taste and a huge ORAC value. The traditional addition of nutmeg is a major feel-good factor, as this exotic spice is a great mood enhancer. This is a sweet thing and not remotely naughty.

75g (3oz) pudding rice
2 teaspoons brown sugar
600ml (1pint) milk
225g (8oz) mixed dried fruits – prunes, apples, mangoes, apricots,
* raisins, sultanas, cranberries, etc., all cut to the size of raisiins*
7.5cm (3in) stick cinnamon
1/2 teaspoon ground nutmeg
110g (4oz) unsalted butter, chopped

1 Preheat the oven to 190°C/375°F/ gas mark 5.

2 Put the rice and sugar into an ovenproof bowl and add the milk and dried fruit.

3 Break the cinnamon stick in 2 and add to the bowl.

4 Sprinkle on the nutmeg and dot with butter.

5 Bake for 1 hour.

ORAC value per serving ★★

fruit jelly

Not just a kids' party favourite, but a highly protective, delicious treat – immensely rich in vitamin C, light and refreshing, so it's perfect after beef stews, roasts or casseroles. Apart from its ORAC value, the vitamin C will make sure you get maximum absorption of iron.

Juice of 1 lemon
2 tablespoons runny honey
300ml (1/2 pint) red grape juice
1 sachet gelatine
75g (3oz) redcurrants
110g (4oz) strawberries, hulled and halved
110g (4oz) raspberries
110g (4oz) blueberries

1 Mix the lemon juice with the honey and grape juice.

2 Sprinkle the gelatine onto 4 tablespoons of hot water (or as packet instructs) and stir briskly until it swells.

3 Line a 450g (1lb) loaf tin with cling film.

4 Strip the fruit off most of the redcurrant stems, leaving 1 or 2 whole for decoration. Arrange in the loaf tin with the other fruit.

5 Heat the gelatine mixture gently until it dissolves, then stir into the grape juice mixture and pour over the fruit.

6 Put into the fridge until set – 1–2 hours, depending on your fridge temperature.

7 Turn out and decorate with the reserved redcurrant stems.

ORAC value per serving ★★★★✔

tea bread with raisins and prunes

The delicate flavour of bergamot oil in the tea, the almost negligible fat content from the egg and the enormous protective benefits of its ORAC score make this a treat you could enjoy without a single pang of conscience.

5 Earl Grey tea bags
300ml (¹/₂ pint) freshly boiled water
1 free-range organic egg, beaten
225g (8oz) raisins
225g (8oz) prunes, cut to the size of raisins
200g (7oz) brown sugar
250g (9oz) organic self-raising flour

1 Soak the tea bags in the water and leave until cold. Squeeze the tea bags and discard.

2 Mix all the ingredients together and leave for at least 6 hours.

3 Preheat the oven to180°C/350°F/gas mark 4.

4 Line a 1.2 litre (2 pint) loaf tin neatly with greaseproof paper. Spoon in the mixture and bake for 30 minutes, or until a skewer inserted into the centre comes out clean.

ORAC value per serving ★★★★

tea bread with dried cherries, cranberries and apricots

The bite of ginger and the tanginess of the lemon and cranberries make this another fabulous tea bread which you can enjoy on its own or as a dessert served with your favourite ice cream or yogurt sauce (see page 126)

5 lemon and ginger tea bags
300ml (¹/₂ pint) boiling water
450g (1lb) mixed dried cherries, cranberries and apricots
1 free-range organic egg, beaten
200g (7oz) brown sugar
250g (9oz) organic self-raising flour

1 Soak the tea bags in the water and leave until cold. Squeeze the tea bags and discard.

2 Quarter the apricots.

3 Mix all the ingredients together and leave for at least 6 hours.

4 Preheat the oven to 180°C/350°F/gas mark 4.

5 Line a 1.2 litre (2 pint) loaf tin neatly with greaseproof paper. Spoon in the mixture and bake for 30 minutes, or until a skewer inserted into the centre comes out clean.

250 ml (9fl oz) elderflower pressé or diluted elderflower cordial
110g (4oz) sugar – but see directions below before adding all of it
1 large mango, cubed
About 200g (7oz) redcurrants, stripped from stems
2 tablespoons lemon juice

1 Put the elderflower pressé or cordial into a saucepan. If the liquid you're using is unsweetened, add all the sugar. If it already has added sugar, use half the amount.

2 Bring slowly to the boil and boil for 4 minutes. Remove from the heat and leave to cool.

3 Meanwhile, mix together enough of the mango and redcurrants to make 450g (1lb). Liquidise and press through a medium sieve.

4 Combine the fruit with the elderflower liquid and lemon juice.

5 If you have an ice-cream maker that also makes sorbets, process according to instructions. If not, pour the mixture into a flattish freezer-proof dish, place in the freezer and leave until almost frozen.

6 Remove from the freezer, break up thoroughly with a fork or whizz in a food processor. Return to the freezer and repeat the process.

7 Leave in the freezer until you have the texture you require, some people like sorbets more solid than others. If yours over-freezes, transfer to the fridge 2 hours before serving.

ORAC value per serving ★✦

mango and redcurrant sorbet

The delicate taste of elderflower, the succulent sweetness of the mango and the acidity of fresh redcurrants combine to give this sorbet its unique flavour. It's an excellent source of betacarotene, vitamin C and ORAC.

ORAC value per serving ★★

passion fruit and blackberry sorbet

Although it's widely used in other parts of the world, rosewater seldom appears in our everyday recipes. What a shame! Its distinctive taste and perfume enhance this unusual sorbet, which contains large amounts of vitamins C and E as well as having a high ORAC score.

Juice of 1 large pink grapefruit
150ml (5fl oz) rosewater
110g (4oz) sugar
6 passion fruit
About 275g (10oz) blackberries

1 Add the grapefruit juice to the rosewater until you have 250ml (9fl oz) of liquid. If it's not enough, add some water.

2 Put the mixture into a pan with the sugar, bring slowly to the boil and boil for 4 minutes. Remove from the heat and leave to cool.

3 Meanwhile, scoop out the passion fruit and sieve into a bowl, discarding the pips.

4 Liquidise the blackberries, sieve to remove the pips and add the purée to the passion fruit to make 450g (1lb) in weight. Mix the fruit into the cooled rosewater liquid.

5 If you have an ice-cream maker that also makes sorbets, process according to instructions. If not, pour the mixture into a flattish freezer-proof dish, place in the freezer and leave until almost frozen.

6 Remove from the freezer, break up thoroughly with a fork or whizz in a food processor. Return to the freezer and repeat the process.

7 Leave in the freezer until you have the texture you require; some people like sorbets more solid than others. If yours over-freezes, transfer to the fridge 2 hours before serving.

ORAC value per serving ★★★

fruit chocolate fondue

Here's the most romantic of desserts, as the theobromine in dark chocolate triggers feelings of love and affection. In spite of the chocolate and a very modest amount of single cream, this is a light and refreshing dessert extremely rich in healing enzymes, minerals and vitamins, and with a very high ORAC score.

1 large mango
1 small pineapple
150g (5oz) small strawberries
2 bananas
1 small bunch red grapes
225g (8oz) good-quality, dark chocolate – preferably organic,
  such as Green and Blacks
125ml (4fl oz) single cream
2 tablespoons kirsch or Grand Marnier

1 First prepare the fruit: cut into bite-sized pieces if necessary, arrange on 4 plates and put into the fridge until you're ready to serve.

2 Cut or break the chocolate into small pieces and put into a fondue pot or small saucepan. Add the cream and cook over a low heat until dissolved. Don't allow it to boil.

3 Stir in the liqueur.

4 If using a fondue set, take it to the table and use the forks to dip the fruit into the chocolate. If you made the fondue in a pan, simply pour the sauce over or beside the fruit and serve immediately.

ORAC value per serving ★★★★★

blueberry and prune muffins

It's hard to believe, but this recipe really works. In fact, you can substitute an equivalent weight of prune purée for fat in most baking recipes. Because of their natural sweetness, you can also reduce the amount of sugar, making these the healthiest muffins you've ever tasted – have two each.

10 large, stoneless, ready-to-eat prunes
175g (6oz) mixed plain and wholemeal flour
2 teaspoons baking powder
25g (1oz) caster sugar
1 free-range organic egg, beaten
150ml (5fl oz) semi-skimmed milk
100g (3¹/₂oz) blueberries

1 Preheat the oven to 200°C/400°F/gas mark 6 and grease 8 deep muffin tins.

2 Make the prune purée by whizzing the prunes in a food processor with a little water until they have the consistency of double cream.

3 Mix together the flours, baking powder and sugar.

4 Mix together the egg, milk and prune purée. Add to the flour mixture and beat thoroughly.

5 Mix in the blueberries, being careful not to break up the fruit.

6 Divide the mixture between the muffin tins, filling only to just over half their depth, and bake for 25 minutes, or until a skewer inserted into the centre comes out clean.

ORAC value per serving ★

pawpaw and couscous pudding

You've probably never eaten couscous as a sweet, as it's nearly always served as a savoury salad, but I strongly recommend this luscious pudding. You'll get lots of betacarotene from the pawpaw, minerals and some vitamin C from the fruit juice, no fat, no added sugar – and it's just as good hot or cold.

450ml (16fl oz) unsweetened cherry juice (or cranberry or unfiltered apple if you can't find it)
110g (4oz) couscous
1 large or 2 small pawpaws, peeled, deseeded and sliced lengthways

1 Put the juice in a large saucepan and bring to a simmer.

2 Add the couscous gradually, allowing it to soak up the liquid. You may need to add a little more or less, depending on the quality of couscous.

3 Serve the couscous hot or cold with the fruit arranged on top.

ORAC value per serving ★★★

honeyed fruit kebabs

I was first served pineapple and cinnamon kebabs by one of London's great Indian chefs at the fabulous Chor Bazaar. This adaptation adds extra nutrients from the raspberries, mango and pawpaw, and although it's a bit more complex, the increase in ORAC score is worth the effort.

1 pineapple
1 large mango, not too ripe
1 large pawpaw, not too ripe
2 bananas
125ml (4fl oz) runny honey
125ml (4fl oz) red grape juice
1/2 teaspoon ground cinnamon
10g (1/2oz) butter
225g (8oz) raspberries

1 Prepare the pineapple, mango, pawpaw and bananas, and cut into evenly sized cubes.

2 Melt the honey in the grape juice in a saucepan over a low heat.

3 Add the cinnamon and butter, stir well until the butter melts, and keep on a very low heat.

4 Thread the pieces of cubed fruit onto kebab sticks. Brush with the honey mixture.

5 Put under a hot grill – or onto a barbecue – and cook for 3 minutes each side. Serve immediately on a bed of raspberries, with any leftover honey mixture poured on top.

ORAC value per serving ★★★✦

prune and chocolate terrine

Everyone needs to sin occasionally, and I could hardly deny that butter, chocolate, eggs, cream and sugar are a bit sinful when you eat them all at once. But as you lick your lips after this amazing dish, you'll know that your indulgence has been tempered with the protective benefits of ORAC.

About 500ml (18fl oz) hot tea
225g (8oz) stone-in prunes
75g (3oz) unsalted butter
175g (6oz) good quality plain chocolate – preferably organic
3 free-range organic eggs, separated
250ml (9fl oz) double cream
25g (1oz) brown caster sugar
30g (1oz) organic cocoa powder
175g (6oz) large, seedless white grapes, halved

1 Pour the tea over the prunes and leave to soak for about 12 hours. Drain and remove the prune stones.

2 Melt the butter gently in a saucepan. Break the chocolate into small pieces and melt gently in the butter.

3 Whisk the egg whites until stiff.

4 Whisk the cream until stiff.

5 Beat the egg yolks, sugar and cocoa together, then add the melted chocolate.

6 Add the cream and egg whites and stir in gently until smooth.

7 Line a 900g (2lb) loaf tin neatly with greaseproof paper and spoon in half the mixture. Arrange half the grapes on top, cover with the prunes, and put the remaining grapes on top of the prunes.

8 Spoon in the remaining chocolate mixture.

9 Freeze until firm – about 6 hours.

10 About 2 hours before serving remove the terrine from the freezer and from the tin and allow to soften.

ORAC value per serving ★★✄

plums baked in red wine and cranberry juice

This is a very simple but different dessert with a variety of health benefits. The cranberry juice helps relieve cystitis, the fresh mint makes it an excellent digestive, the red wine is good for your heart and the plums provide fibre, vitamins and minerals.

50g (2oz) unsalted butter
8 plump red plums, halved and stoned
450ml (16fl oz) mixed red wine and cranberry juice
4 large sprigs mint, finely chopped
4 tablespoons brown caster sugar

1 Preheat the oven to 180°C/350°F/ gas mark 4.

2 Rub the bottom of a shallow casserole dish with half the butter. Sprinkle with half the sugar and lay the plums on top, cut side down. Pour over the wine and cranberry juice, and sprinkle with the mint.

3 Dot the rest of the butter on top and dust with the remaining sugar.

4 Bake for 20 minutes.

ORAC value per serving ★ﾉ

prune soufflé

Don't be nervous about soufflés and don't worry if they don't always turn out right – I've seen great chefs take a dish of collapsed goo out of the oven. This dish really is worth a try, as the texture and flavour are remarkable and the wafting aroma of alcoholic coffee will make your mouth water long before you take the first spoonful.

110g (4oz) ready-to-eat prunes
25g (1oz) chopped mixed nuts
35g (1¹/₂oz) fresh breadcrumbs
1 tablespoon soft brown sugar
¹/₂ level teaspoon allspice
Grated rind of ¹/₂ lemon
1 tablespoon lemon juice
1 tablespoon Tia Maria
2 free-range organic eggs, separated

1 Preheat the oven to 180°C/350°F/gas mark 4, and lightly grease a 1.2 litre (2 pint) soufflé dish.

2 Boil the prunes in just enough water to cover for 10 minutes. Drain, reserving the liquid. Whizz the prunes in a food processor until smooth.

3 Mix the nuts, breadcrumbs, sugar and allspice in a large bowl, then stir in the prune mixture. Mix in the lemon rind and lemon juice, Tia Maria and egg yolks.

4 Stir in 75ml (3fl oz) of the prune liquid, making up the quantity with water if necessary.

5 Whisk the egg whites until stiff and gently fold into the prune mixture. Spoon the mixture into the soufflé dish and bake for 40 minutes or until risen. Serve immediately.

ORAC value per serving ★★★★

ORAC brulée

The ultimate healthy indulgence – go on, you deserve it! And with its enormous ORAC rating, it will do you good too.

900g (2lb) mixed blueberries, blackberries, strawberries, raspberries and cherries (stoned)
300ml (¹/₂ pint) double cream
250g (9oz) natural bio-yogurt – preferably organic
4 tablespoons demerara sugar

1 Put the fruit into one large ovenproof dish or 4 large –10cm (4in) – individual ovenproof ramekins.

2 Beat the cream until thick, then mix in the yogurt thoroughly. Spread this mixture over the fruit, covering it completely. Sprinkle the sugar over the top.

3 Put under a very hot grill until the sugar is caramelised – 3–5 minutes.

4 Allow to cool slightly before serving or leave in the fridge and serve cold.

juices & smoothies

All recipes in this chapter make 2 large glasses.

juices

In terms of health, flavour, nutrition and ORAC scores, fresh, home-made juices come out top in every respect. Most kitchens today will have some kind of liquidiser, blender or food processor, even if it is stuck away in an inaccessible cupboard. And you need one of these to make smoothies.

Unfortunately, they're no good for juices and, in my experience, juicing attachments for multi-purpose machines are a waste of space and money. They're not very efficient, they're fiddly, create lots of washing up and seldom get used. Dedicated juicers are now easily available and come in two types: centrifugal and masticating. If you've never juiced before, start with an inexpensive centrifugal machine. All the leading manufacturers, such as Braun, Phillips and Kenwood, have decent models at reasonable prices.

Centrifugal machines spin the residue into a container or filter and in small machines this limits how much juice you can make before having to stop and clean it out. More expensive but more efficient is the Waring Professional in fashionable stainless steel, with a much larger filter – and it produces more juice. My favourite juicer of this type is the American Superjuicer, which is fairly quiet, efficient, easy to clean and has the great advantage of throwing the pulp out of the machine and into a plastic bag. You can make as much as you want without stopping and the pulp is ready just to chuck on the compost pile, if you have one.

Masticating juicers crush the fruit and vegetables between stainless steel rollers and are the most efficient of all. They run at lower temperatures, which protects the enzymes, extract much more of the juice and push the pulp out of the other end of the machine. They'll take frozen fruits to make instant sorbets, grind nuts and seeds – you can make your own peanut butter – and some of them will even grind flour. They are, naturally, much more expensive and bulkier, but if you're a serious juicer, invest in one of these and you have a machine that will last a lifetime. I use two of the best machines – the Champion and Green Life, both of which come from the USA.

You'll have seen a list of the highest ORAC foods in the general introduction. The recipes in this chapter are just suggestions – with many of my own favourites – but they're not set in stone. Use your imagination and cater to your own family tastes. Be bold and experiment, as some of the most surprising combinations end up tasting great. Juicing is the perfect way to persuade anyone – particularly children – who's not that keen on vegetables or fruits to make up the minimum of five portions a day. My own wife, who goes green at the sight of a beetroot, was finally persuaded to taste one of my strange mixtures and has been hooked ever since.

The recipes given here will make two large glasses, but the proportions are just a guideline and the amount of juice you get will depend on the individual ingredients – how fresh, how ripe, how juicy. But if you have, for example, only one kiwi, add another apple. If there are only two pears in your bowl, but you've got a bag full of carrots, just keep juicing until you have enough, even though the juice might be orange rather than green. It really doesn't matter, as a glass of freshly juiced produce will be a cornucopia of vitamins, minerals, enzymes, valuable plant chemicals and, most importantly, ORAC.

Just a word about preparing your fruit and vegetables for juicing. It depends very much on the type of machine you're using, so look at the instructions. There's no need to peel or core apples or pears and you don't need to remove the skin from any fruit or vegetables, even kiwis. The more robust juicers will even cope with unpeeled pineapples. If you're using organic produce, just wash well before juicing, but if they're not organic, wash in warm water with 1 teaspoon of washing-up liquid per 1 litre (1³/4 pints). Scrub hard vegetables and fruits and, obviously, be more gentle with soft fruits and make sure you rinse well. Non-organic carrots should be topped and tailed, and if you're juicing for children, I'd recommend peeling them to be on the safe side.

Most machines will juice citrus fruits such as oranges and grapefruit if you peel them first, but thin-skinned tangerines and lemons can be used unpeeled, although this does give a slightly bitter tang to the finished juice. Anything with a very tough skin, such as avocados, passion fruit, mangoes, or pawpaws, will need to be peeled and any large central stones or seeds removed. Mango skin can cause contact allergies – mangos are related to the poison ivy – so if you're preparing lots of them at the same time, it's sensible to wear thin gloves.

ORAC value per glass ★★★

kiwi, raspberry and blueberry

2 large kiwi fruit
110g (4oz) mixed raspberries and blueberries
250ml (9fl oz) unfiltered organic apple juice
250ml (9fl oz) cranberry juice

ORAC value per glass ★★✦

carrot, apple and kiwi

4 large carrots
3 good-flavoured eating apples – Cox's are the best
3 kiwi fruit

ORAC value per glass ★

carrot, sweet potato and celery

4 large carrots
2 sweet potatoes
3 sticks celery

ORAC value per glass ★

beetroot, apple and carrot

1 beetroot, with leaves
2 apples
3 carrots

ORAC value per glass ★★✦

cucumber, beetroot and chard

1 cucumber
1 beetroot
110g (4oz) Swiss chard or baby spinach

ORAC value per glass ★★

tomato, celery, radish and red pepper

4 large tomatoes
3 sticks celery
12 radishes
1 red pepper

ORAC value per glass ★✦

pear, apple and blueberry

3 Conference pears
2 large dessert apples
115g (4oz) blueberries

ORAC value per glass ★★★

orange, carrot, spinach and ginger

2 large oranges
1 carrot
110g (4oz) baby spinach
2.5cm (1in) fresh ginger, peeled

ORAC value per glass ★★★

strawberry, blueberry, cranberry and red grape

110g (4oz) strawberries
110g (4oz) blueberries
110g (4oz) defrosted frozen cranberries
110g (4oz) seedless red grapes

ORAC value per glass ★★★★★

prune, apple, blackberry and mango

10 ready-to-eat prunes soaked in 300ml (10fl oz) apple juice
  overnight
110g (4oz) blackberries
1 mango

ORAC value per glass ★★★

orange, pink grapefruit, lime and raspberry

2 oranges
1 pink grapefruit
2 limes
110g (4oz) raspberries

ORAC value per glass ✒

blueberry, cranberry and blackcurrant cooler

110g (4oz) blueberries
110g (4oz) defrosted frozen cranberries
110g (4oz) blackcurrants
A handful of ice cubes

ORAC value per glass ✒

traditional bellini

3 large, pink peaches
1/2 bottle iced champagne

Juice the peaches. Pour into flutes and top with champagne

smoothies

Making smoothies couldn't be simpler. All you need is a blender, liquidiser or food processor, your choice of prepared fresh fruit, soft vegetables or salad ingredients and a milk- or soya-based liquid to bind it all together. All the ingredients are liquidised together in a matter of minutes. If you have a juicer, you can make your own juice from tougher vegetables like carrots; if you haven't, there are several ranges of excellent commercially prepared organic vegetable juices in most supermarkets. Smoothies are ideal if you're having problems getting enough fruit into your diet – or, more importantly, your children's. From a kids'-health point of view, these creamy drinks made at home are about as far as you can get from the commercially made chemical-ridden shakes they get in burger bars – and they're just as delicious. You can vary the texture and consistency to suit your or your family's preferences. Thick enough to eat with a spoon or thin enough to drink through a straw – it's entirely up to you. Add a scoop of the kids' favourite ice cream, throw in a few ice cubes while blending or, for the adults, turn them into sophisticated 'smoothtails' by adding a measure of any of the sweet liqueurs: cherry brandy, Cointreau, crème de menthe, Galliano or Kahlua. You could also throw in a slug of vodka, gin, Jack Daniels or whatever spirit takes your fancy.

Smoothies provide lots of energy, loads of vitamin C, a quarter of your daily calcium requirement, and those based on yogurt also provide plenty of the good bugs that make your digestion work more efficiently and boost your natural immunity.

As with the juices earlier in this chapter, the recipes here are just a selection of my particular favourites and ideas given to me by friends and, very often, my patients. Smoothies are a great way to experiment with flavours – and kids love to come up with something that is theirs and theirs alone.

ORAC value per glass ★★★

strawberry, banana and blueberry

4 large strawberries
1 small banana
110g (4oz) blueberries
425g (15oz) natural bio-yogurt

ORAC value per glass ★★

banana, strawberry, kiwi, milk and honey

1 banana
110g (4oz) strawberries
2 kiwi fruit
600ml (1 pint) full-fat milk
2 tablespoons honey

ORAC value per glass ★★★★

soya milk, prune juice and blueberry

250ml (9fl oz) soya milk
125ml (4fl oz) unsweetened prune juice
  (shop bought or make your own)
110g (4oz) blueberries

ORAC value per glass ★★

kiwi, cherry, grape and yogurt

3 kiwi fruit
75g (3oz) fresh cherries (stoneless weight)
110g (4oz) white seedless grapes
425g (15oz) natural bio-yogurt

ORAC value per glass ★★★

avocado, pawpaw, yogurt, chilli and mint

2 large avocados
1 large pawpaw
425g (15oz) natural bio-yogurt
3 small, fresh red chillies, deseeded
6 large mint leaves

ORAC value per glass ★

passion fruit, pineapple, banana and yogurt

6 passion fruit, pressed firmly through a sieve to get rid of the pips
1 small or 1/2 large pineapple
2 bananas
425g (15oz) natural bio-yogurt

ORAC value per glass ★

pineapple, mango, banana and coconut milk

1 small pineapple
1 mango
2 bananas
400ml (14fl oz) canned coconut milk

ORAC value per glass ★★

apple, pear, plum, yogurt, and honey

3 dessert apples
2 Conference pears
6 plums
400g (14oz) natural bio-yogurt
2 tablespoons runny honey

ORAC value per glass ★

beetroot, cucumber, yogurt, mint and garlic

2 small, cooked beetroot, finely cubed
1/2 cucumber, peeled and deseeded
400g (14oz) natural bio-yogurt
20 mint leaves
2 garlic cloves

ORAC value per glass ★★

banana, strawberry and blueberry

1 small banana
75g (3oz) strawberries
110g (4oz) blueberries
425g (15oz) live natural yogurt

ORAC value per glass ★

pineapple, mango, pawpaw with soya milk and ginger

1 pineapple
1 mango
1 pawpaw
600ml (1 pint) soya milk
2.5cm (1in.) peeled ginger root

sauces, marinades & compôtes

All the recipes in this book have valuable ORAC scores, but using these sauces and extras will give them a valuable boost. In addition, adding them to any of your other favourite recipes, even those with low scores, will help boost their ORAC rating and increase the life-protecting value of your cooking.

savoury sauces

ORAC value per average serving ⤴

fresh tomato sauce

The huge concentration of lycopene in tomato purée, combined with canned tomatoes and carrot, makes this an all-round savoury sauce or dip.

4 tablespoons olive oil
6 tablespoons tomato purée
450g (16oz) canned organic crushed tomatoes
1/2 teaspoon caster sugar
1 carrot, grated
Leaves of 4 large sprigs fresh basil, roughly torn
Salt and pepper

1 Heat the oil in a saucepan.

2 Stir in the tomato purée, crushed tomatoes and sugar.

3 Add the carrot and simmer for 25 minutes, adding water if the sauce gets too thick.

4 Add the basil and simmer for another 5 minutes.

5 Taste and adjust seasoning.

ORAC value per average serving ◢

spicy tomato sauce

With loads of lycopene and the blood-positive qualities of garlic and onions, this makes a great sauce or dip.

2 tablespoons safflower oil
30g (1oz) unsalted butter
1 onion, finely chopped
2 garlic cloves, finely chopped
3 small red chillies, deseeded and finely chopped
450g (16oz) canned organic crushed tomatoes

1 Heat the oil and butter in a saucepan, add the onion and garlic, and sauté them gently, stirring occasionally, until soft – about 10 minutes.

2 Add the chillies and the tomatoes to the onion mixture. Simmer gently until the mixture thickens.

ORAC value per average serving ◢

hot tomato salsa

Extra hot and spicy, this healthy salsa is ideal as a dip or accompaniment to hot or cold dishes.

3 large tomatoes
1 red onion, very finely chopped
2 large red chillies, deseeded and finely chopped
Leaves of 3 sprigs fresh coriander, finely chopped
4 tablespoons tomato purée

1 Peel the tomatoes by placing them in a bowl of boiling water for 2 minutes until the skins start to come away and can be slipped off easily. Chop finely.

2 Mix the tomatoes, onion, chillies, coriander and tomato purée together in a bowl and leave in the fridge to chill for 1 hour.

ORAC value per average serving ★◢

special apple sauce

An ideal accompaniment to hot or cold dishes, and equally at home in a pancake, mixed with yogurt, rice pudding or your breakfast cereal.

1kg (2¼lb) cooking apples, cored, peeled and sliced
150ml (5fl oz) water
110g (4oz) raisins, washed
6 whole cloves
1 tablespoon brown sugar
20g (¾oz) unsalted butter

1 Place the apples in a saucepan with the water.

2 Add the raisins, cloves and sugar, and simmer the mixture gently until mushy, then fish out the cloves.

3 Beat the mixture to a pulp and stir in the butter.

ORAC value per average serving ★★

cranberry sauce

A traditional sauce with turkey, pâté or game.

500g (18oz) fresh or frozen and thawed cranberries
3 tablespoons brown sugar
150ml (5fl oz) water

1 Wash the cranberries and pick them over carefully.

2 Beat lightly with a wooden spoon until bruised.

3 Simmer in the water and sugar until tender.

4 Push through a sieve to remove the skins and pips.

ORAC value per average serving ★⌐

gooseberry sauce

This simple and delicious sauce is equally at home on hot or cold, sweet or savoury dishes – and it makes a fabulous topping for ice cream. The highest ORAC value is obtained by using sweet, red dessert gooseberries.

500g (18oz) ripe gooseberries, washed and picked over
600ml (1 pint) water or any wine you may have left over
3–4 tablespoons brown sugar
A generous knob unsalted butter
2 tablespoons Calvados (optional)

1 Place the gooseberries.in a saucepan with the water or wine and simmer until soft.

2 Push through a sieve to remove the skins. Return to the pan and add the sugar to taste and the butter.

3 Reheat and stir in the Calvados.

ORAC value per average serving ★

horseradish sauce

Rich in highly protective sulphur compounds, horseradish is the perfect accompaniment to hot or cold roast beef and smoked fish. It's really worth growing your own or buying fresh roots when they're available. Grated and frozen, it will keep all its flavour and health properties, and although used only as a condiment, one tablespoon is a good addition to your daily ORAC consumption.

250ml (9fl oz) double or whipping cream
6 tablespoons grated horseradish – if you grow it or can find some growing wild and do it yourself, all the better
3 tablespoons white wine vinegar or cider vinegar
Salt and pepper

1 Whisk the cream to thicken it.

2 Stir in the horseradish and vinegar.

3 Taste and add salt and/or pepper if necessary.

ORAC value per average serving ★✈

horseradish and beetroot sauce

This traditional Eastern European recipe is perfect with cold meats and strongly flavoured fish. The combination of high-value beetroot with horseradish makes it extra protective.

2 large cooked (not pickled) beetroots, finely grated
150g (5oz) grated horseradish – buy it prepared or grate the raw
   root yourself
About 2 tablespoons brown caster sugar
Red wine vinegar

1 Place the beetroots in a bowl, add the grated horseradish and mix well.

2 Stir in the sugar, tasting – carefully, as it will be very hot on its own – until the sweetness suits your palate.

3 Gradually beat in just enough vinegar as will to bind the sauce.

ORAC value per average serving ★

orange sauce

This really easy-to-make and delicately sweet-and-sour sauce is ideal with duck, goose, venison or smoked sausage. It's rich in vitamin C and has good ORAC value, too.

Grated rind and juice of 3 oranges
150g (5oz) redcurrant jelly
3 tablespoons brown sugar
Juice of 1 lemon
2 pinches paprika
3 tablespoons port or brandy

1 Whizz the orange rind, redcurrant jelly and sugar in a blender.

2 Pour the mixture into a saucepan, add the orange and lemon juices, paprika and port or brandy, and heat through, adding more paprika for a spicier taste.

ORAC value per average serving ★

cumberland sauce

This is a traditional sauce, usually served with coarse terrines and cold pies, like game, pork or veal and ham. I think it also goes well with strong cheeses, such as a really mature organic farmhouse Cheddar or red Leicester.

Grated rind and juice of 2 oranges
Grated rind and juice of 2 lemons
2 tablespoons mild mustard
1 tablespoon brown caster sugar
100ml (3 1/2 fl oz) redcurrant jelly
1/2 teaspoon cayenne pepper
50ml (2fl oz) red wine
2 tablespoons port

1 Simmer the grated orange and lemon rind in water until softened – about 4 minutes. Drain.

2 Put the orange and lemon juices in another pan. Add the grated rind, mustard, sugar, redcurrant jelly, cayenne pepper and wine. Simmer very gently for about 5 minutes, adding more wine if the mixture gets too thick.

3 Stir in the port.

sweet sauces

raspberry sauce

Nothing quite matches the taste of raspberries, and when combined with the health-giving benefits of pro-biotic bacteria in live yogurt, the result is a delicious, immune-boosting, high-ORAC sauce.

350g (12oz) raspberries, washed and hulled – fresh are obviously
*   best, frozen will do, but canned most certainly won't*
4 tablespoons kirsch or any raspberry liqueur
Icing sugar
75g (3oz) natural bio-yogurt, preferably organic (optional)

1 Whizz the raspberries with the liqueur in a blender or mash the two together thoroughly with a fork. Push through a fine sieve to remove the pips.

2 If you like a very tart sauce, forget the sugar. Otherwise sweeten the sauce to taste.

3 If you want to make a slightly creamy sauce, stir in the yogurt.

yogurt sauce

Good enough to eat on its own, but wonderful served with hot or cold desserts, this sauce has good bugs, vitamin C and all the digestive benefits of mint.

150g (5oz) blackcurrants, washed and hulled
Grated rind of 1 lemon
2 tablespoons honey
1/2 teaspoon ground cinnamon
1 large sprig mint, finely chopped
250g (9oz) natural bio-yogurt, preferably organic

1 Place the blackcurrants in a saucepan with water to cover and simmer gently for 5–10 minutes until just tender. Drain and push the berries through a fine sieve to remove the pips. Leave the purée to cool completely.

2 Mix the lemon rind, honey, cinnamon and mint into the yogurt.

3 When the blackcurrant purée is cold, stir it thoroughly into the yogurt mixture.

★★

three-fruit sauce

With the lemon juice taking the edge off the sweetness, this sauce is best served warm with hot or cold desserts. It's especially wonderful poured over vanilla ice cream or used on hot waffles or pancakes. Not surprisingly, it turns any pudding into an ORAC feast.

110g (4oz) dried apricots
110g (4oz) dried, stoneless prunes
110g (4oz) fresh or frozen cranberries
Juice of 3 lemons

1 Put the dried fruit and the cranberries into a large saucepan and just cover with boiling water. Bring back to the boil, cover, and simmer until tender, checking regularly that the mixture isn't drying out.

2 Transfer the fruit with about 100ml (3½fl oz) of the water to a blender and whizz to a purée. (Depending on the size of your blender, you may have to do this in batches.) Reserve the remainder of the cooking water.

3 Return the purée to a dry saucepan, adding more of the cooking water if it seems too thick. Heat through and stir in the lemon juice.

★★★

blueberry sauce

Of all grapes, the American Concord has the highest ORAC value. Mixed here with another top-ranking anti-oxidant food, blueberries, it provides enormous health benefits that more than make up for the small amount of sugar – whatever 'naughty' pudding you decide to pour this over. It's equally good hot or cold on ice-cream, apple pie or rice pudding.

250g (9oz) blueberries
250ml (9fl oz) American Concord red grape juice
1 tablespoon organic Demerara sugar
2 pinches nutmeg

1 Just whizz all the ingredients together.

marinades

peanut marinade and sauce

Some of the marinade will be absorbed by the food soaking in it. To get the full ORAC value, add the rest of the marinade during the cooking process. If using meat or fish, cook at a sufficiently high temperature to boil the added marinade and kill any bacteria that may have seeped from these foods.

100ml (3¹/₂fl oz) basic stock (see page ??)
4 heaped tablespoons smooth peanut butter
2 tablespoons soy sauce
3 garlic cloves
3 tablespoons rice vinegar or white wine vinegar
2 teaspoons brown sugar
Leaves of 2 large sprigs coriander, roughly chopped
Leaves of 2 large sprigs flat-leaf parsley, roughly chopped
¹/₂ teaspoon cayenne pepper

1 Bring the stock gently to the boil.

2 Place in a blender with the peanut butter, soy sauce and garlic, and whizz until smooth.

3 Add the vinegar and sugar, and whizz again for 10 seconds.

4 Put the mixture into the rinsed-out saucepan. Add the herbs with the cayenne pepper and heat through.

mandarin's marinade

This hot recipe can be used as a marinade for meat, fish or poultry, but is equally valuable as a hot pouring sauce. You can keep it covered in the fridge for three or four days. This unmistakably oriental mixture isn't an exceptionally high ORAC recipe, but has the bonus of being a great circulatory booster.

10cm (4in.) fresh root ginger, peeled and finely grated
Juice of 1 orange
*300ml (10fl oz) basic stock (see page ??) or stock made with a
    low-salt, preferably organic, stock cube*
75ml (3fl oz) hoisin sauce
3 tablespoons light soy sauce
6 tablespoons rice vinegar
3 tablespoons extra-virgin olive oil
3 tablespoons sesame seed oil
5 teaspoons mild mustard

1 Put all the ingredients into a blender and whizz until smooth.

`ORAC value per average serving` ⌐

basic meat marinade

As well as imparting flavour and ORAC value, these marinades actually start the cooking process and help to tenderise meat and poultry. Both mint and tarragon are excellent digestive herbs and provide extra ORAC.

3 garlic cloves, very finely chopped
1 sprig rosemary, finely chopped
A few sprigs thyme, finely chopped
A few sprigs marjoram, finely chopped
250ml (9fl oz) red wine
250ml (9fl oz) extra-virgin olive oil

1 Mix the garlic and herbs into the wine and oil.

2 Baste the meat in the mixture and leave in the fridge for at least 2 hours.

3 Add the meat and marinade to casseroles or strain off the marinade, grill, roast or barbecue the meat and use the marinade as a baste or in a sauce or gravy.

For lamb*: add 2 large stems mint*
For poultry*: add 4 stems tarragon*

`ORAC value per average serving` ⌐

marinade for fish

Marinating fish helps to bring out the wonderful flavours that are unique to each variety, and, in spite of the mixture of herbs, the marinades won't dominate the taste of your finished dish. The combination of herbs, capers and lemon produce the ORAC score in this marinade.

1 teaspoon capers, drained
Milk
1 lemon
250ml (9fl oz) white wine
250ml (9fl oz) light virgin olive oil
6 sprigs dill
3 sprigs chervil
2 sprigs parsley

1 Place the capers in enough milk to cover them and soak for 10 minutes – this removes any excessive sharpness. Drain and squash lightly. Finely grate the rind from the lemon and cut the fruit into slices.

2 Mix the wine and olive oil in a bowl. Add the capers and lemon rind and stir thoroughly. Stir in the whole sprigs of dill, chervil and parsley.

3 Pour the marinade over the fish, top with the lemon slices and leave in the fridge for 1 hour.

4 If you're grilling the fish or putting it on a barbecue, drain from the marinade, put on or under the heat and use the juices as a baste. If you're baking, roasting or casseroling, use as much of the marinade as you like for flavour in the stock, in fish cooked in pockets of foil, or boiled down to make a sauce.

compôtes

All these compôtes have high-ORAC scores and can make a considerable difference to your daily ORAC intake. It's nice to know that these delicious sweet additions to your favourite dishes have such wonderful health benefits.

ORAC value per average serving ★★✔	ORAC value per average serving ★★✔
## dried fruit compôte	## fresh berry compôte

This is perfect with cold meats, poultry and strong cheeses.

250g (9oz) mixed dried prunes, apricots and sultanas
Finely grated rind and juice of 1 lemon
400ml (14fl oz) sweet white wine
3 cinnamon sticks

1 Put the dried fruit, lemon juice and rind into a large saucepan and cover with the wine.

2 Add the cinnamon sticks and simmer gently until the fruit is tender.

3 Remove the cinnamon sticks before serving.

The French think we're a bit strange eating 'jam' with meat, but they eat snails and frogs' legs, and no amount of confiture would make me eat those. This cômpote is wonderful with pâté, cold game pie, goose, venison, ham – and, best of all, with cold turkey on Boxing Day, when you need all the ORAC you can get to make up for all the Christmas indulgences.

500g (18oz) mixed fresh or frozen and thawed blackberries,
* raspberries and redcurrants*
4 tablespoons organic honey

1 Wash and pick over the fruit. Put it into a saucepan and add just enough water to cover.

2 Add the honey. Simmer, stirring gently, for 2 minutes to melt the honey, then boil until most of the liquid has evaporated.

ORAC value per average serving ★

rhubarb, ginger and gooseberry compôte

This is actually good enough to eat on its own. But it's also perfect with hot or cold oily fish, smoked fish; stirred into yogurt; poured, hot or cold, over your favourite ice cream; or mixed into muesli for breakfast. For a real treat, serve with hot, home-made apple pie.

200g (7oz) rhubarb, tough fibres removed, stems cut into 1cm
  (1/2in) slices
150g (5oz) gooseberries, stems removed
3cm (1 1/4in.) ginger root, peeled and very finely grated
2 tablespoons runny honey
500ml (18fl oz) unsweetened elderflower cordial, diluted
  if necessary

1 Put the fruit, ginger and honey into a saucepan with just enough elderflower cordial to cover. Simmer until the fruit is tender, adding more cordial if the compôte becomes too dry.

ORAC value per average serving ★★★◢

warm cinnamon compôte

Like all dried fruits, this delicious mixture is exceptionally high in ORAC values. It also has the added digestive bonus of the spice and high fibre content.

1 medium cinnamon stick
2cm (1in) peeled and finely grated ginger root
2 thin slices lemon
75g (3oz) each dried cranberries, blueberries, cherries,baby figs
  and Muscatelle raisins

1 Put all the ingredients into a large bowl and cover with boiling water.

2 Soak for an hour at room temperature.

3 Fish out the lemon slices and serve alone or with yogurt sauce (see page 126).

salad dressings

standard french dressing

Despite the enormous influence of Mediterranean and oriental cooking everywhere in the media, getting a decent salad is still a comparative rarity – and a true delight when you do. The secret is in the preparation and the dressing. Wash all salad ingredients well – even those in the plastic bags that say 'washed and ready to use' – and dry thoroughly. A salad spinner is the best and cheapest kitchen gadget you'll ever buy. Even the best dressing won't coat the surface of wet leaves and you end up with a soggy mess. This dressing will go with any type of salad.

150ml (5fl oz) extra-virgin olive oil
50ml (2fl oz) herb vinegar – make your own by putting a mixture
 of sprigs of rosemary, chervil, parsley and tarragon into
 a bottle and leaving for a least 1 week – or buy commercially
 produced herb vinegar

2 teaspoons mild mustard
1 teaspoon sea salt
3 generous twists freshly ground black pepper
3 tablespoons chopped mixed fresh soft herb leaves – flat-leaf
 parsley, tarragon, marjoram, chervil and oregano

1 Place all the ingredients except the fresh herbs in a bowl and whisk until thickened.

2 Stir in the fresh herbs.

This dressing will keep in an air-tight jar for at least 1 week, but don't put it in the fridge, because it will separate.

ORAC value per average serving ★

creamy yogurt dressing

This cool, green dressing goes well with cold new potatoes, a mixed green leaf salad or cold fresh salmon.

3 tablespoons olive oil
240g (9oz) natural bio-yogurt, preferably organic
1/2 cucumber, peeled, deseeded and finely chopped
1 large green pepper, deseeded and finely diced
1 sweet white Spanish onion, finely chopped
2 garlic cloves, finely chopped

1 Mix the yogurt and olive oil together.

2 Put all the ingredients into a blender and whizz for 1 minute.

ORAC value per average serving ⤏

spicy dressing for fish salads

This refreshing dressing is perfect with any salad made with canned, fresh or smoked tuna, or flaked steamed cod, salmon, trout or mackerel. It's also superb on seafood salads with prawns, crab, lobster, squid or mussels.

125ml (4fl oz) olive oil
125ml (4fl oz) walnut oil
2 small red chillies, deseeded and finely chopped
3 large spring onions, trimmed and finely sliced
1 garlic clove, chopped
2.5cm (1in) fresh ginger, peeled and grated

1 Mix all the ingredients together and leave in the fridge for 1 hour to allow the flavours to combine.

ORAC value per average serving ⤏

thai dressing

Healthy eating is as much about enjoyment as it is about nutrition. Although this oriental combo doesn't have a particularly high ORAC score, it's reasonably high in anti-oxidants and extremely high in heart-protective mono-unsaturated oils, vitamin E and essential trace minerals – and it tastes brilliant on pan-fried or barbecued prawns or chicken.

2 tablespoons oyster sauce
2 tablespoons lemon juice
2 teaspoons runny honey
4 large spring onions, finely chopped
Half a teaspoon paprika
1 tablespoon dry-fried sesame seeds
4 tablespoons sesame oil
2 tablespoons tahini

1 Put all the ingredients into a blender and whizz until smooth, adding more oil if necessary.

7 days of ORACle eating

If you really want to do everything you can to help your food ensure your continuing good health there are 150 ideas in this book. It would be easy to keep your ORAC rating extremely high by eating only, say, the top five foods in the ORAC table. However, confining your food intake to prunes, raisins, blueberries, blackberries and garlic wouldn't just be extremely dull, but you'd be missing out dangerously on a whole range of nutrients which make up the complex needs the body has to keep it running efficiently.

Food should be about enjoyment as much as anything else, but if you can make small changes to your diet, you can enjoy the fun as well as the health benefits. Here's a week of ORAC eating chosen to maximise your consumption of these vital foods without sacrificing the wide range of flavours and textures, which would be anathema to anyone who loves food. And remember, the ORAC values here don't take into account any additional vegetables, potatoes or salads you serve with these dishes.

		page no.	ORAC value

day 1

Breakfast:	Porridge with prunes and raisins	22	6^1/$_2$
	Carrot, apple and kiwi juice	114	2^1/$_2$
Light meal:	Vegetable risotto	59	2^1/$_2$
	Mediterranean mix	55	3
Main meal:	Steamed fish in foil	95	2^1/$_2$
	Plums baked in wine and cranberry juice	108	1^1/$_2$
		Total	**18^1/$_2$ stars**

day 2

Breakfast:	Fruity starter with a poach-up	22	3
Light meal:	Tomato, mozzarella and avocado salad	73	4
	Tea bread with raisins and prunes	102	4^1/$_2$
Main meal:	Cabbage and beetroot soup	43	4
	Stir-fried vegetables with prawns	96	3^1/$_2$
		Total	**19 stars**

		page no.	ORAC value

day 3

Breakfast:	Avocado with sliced tomato	23	2$\frac{1}{2}$
	Orange, pink grapefruit, lime and		
	raspberry juice	115	3
Light meal:	Stuffed red peppers	62	3
	Strawberry, banana and blueberry smoothie	117	3
Main meal:	Braised duck with prunes	90	7
	Watercress, chicory and alfalfa salad	52	4
		Total	**22$\frac{1}{2}$ stars**

day 4

Breakfast:	Fruit-filled melon shells	25	4
Light meal:	Prawn couscous with raisins	66	2$\frac{1}{2}$
	Blueberry and prune muffins	105	5
Main meal:	Mango chicken	79	2$\frac{1}{2}$
	Tabbouleh with a difference	51	1$\frac{1}{2}$	Fruity rice pudding
		100	5
		Total	**20$\frac{1}{2}$ stars**

		page no.	*ORAC value*

day 5

Breakfast:	Swiss muesli with blueberries	24	5
	Strawberry, blueberry, cranberry and red grape juice	115	3
Light meal:	Broccoli and cauliflower cheese	59	3
	Beetroot, pink grapefruit and red onion salad	46	2
Main meal:	Curried bean and root vegetable stew	89	3
	Chilled cherry soup	39	4
		Total	**20 stars**

day 6

Breakfast:	Compôte of dried fruits with yogurt and flax seeds	27	6
Light meal:	Tuna fishcakes	68	2
	Wild and red rice on radicchio	48	1$\frac{1}{2}$
Main meal:	Cheat's gazpacho	34	2$\frac{1}{2}$
	Vegetarian nutty bake	83	3$\frac{1}{2}$
	Prune and chocolate terrine	107	3$\frac{1}{2}$
		Total	**19 stars**

		page no.	ORAC value

day 7

Breakfast: Devilled prunes with spicy tomato sauce   25   6$\frac{1}{2}$
Kiwi, raspberry and blueberry juice   114   3

Light meal: Traditional salade Niçoise   49   1
Blueberry, cranberry and blackcurrant cooler   115   3

Main meal: Cream of broccoli and Brussels sprouts soup   40   2
ORAC brulée   109   4

Total   **19$\frac{1}{2}$ stars**

index of recipes

acknowledgements

I'd like to dedicate this book to my wife Sally, as without her support during my long and tedious recovery from an accident, it would never have been written. She also developed and tested all the recipes, as well as cooking and styling the food for the photographs.

I'd also like to thank Ray Main and his assistant Leigh for taking such fabulous pictures, and Marie-Hélène Jeeves for her cartoons. Needless to say, without the encouragement of Kyle Cathie and her staff, and the untiring efforts of my secretary Janet, *The ORACle Diet* would not exist.

Finally, a special thank you to one of the unsung heroes of healthy eating. Sham Grimshaw runs one of the best wholesale companies at New Covent Garden Market and supplies some of the best chefs and grandest dining rooms in London. I'm happy to say that he has also supplied me with the freshest, healthiest and most delicious selection of every imaginable type of fruit, vegetable, herb and salad.

First published in Great Britain in 2002 by
Kyle Cathie Limited
122 Arlington Road
London NW1 7HP
general.enquiries@kyle-cathie.com
www.kylecathie.com

ISBN 1 85626 459 9

Text © Michael van Straten 2002
Layout © Kyle Cathie Limited 2002
Drawings © Marie-Hélène Jeeves 2002
Photographs © Ray Main 2002

Michael van Straten is hereby identified as the author of this work in accordance with Section 77 of the Copyright, Designs and Patents Act 1998.

A CIP catalogue record for this title is available from the British Library.

Edited by Barbara Horn
Designed by Geoff Hayes
Production by Lorraine Baird and Sha Huxtable

Colour separations by Colourscan
Printed and bound in Singapore by KHL Printing Co. Pte.Ltd.